Fallen Star

The history of Swissair and predecessors

ISBN 978-0-9573744-6-1

Design and layout by Graham Hobster, Moncton, Canada

Introduction

Air transport in the small land-locked country of Switzerland, a territory dominated by lakes and high Alpine mountains began soon after World War One, initially with wartime aircraft and a focus on mail and tourism. Several airlines emerged, based at Zurich, Geneva and Basle, but the Great Depression, which began with the Wall Street Crash in October 1929 and spread throughout Europe and elsewhere, left the airlines severely exposed and led to a retrenchment, further exacerbated by a reduction in subsidies from the Swiss Government. This led to the eventual consolidation and the birth of a new national airline in 1931, the Schweizerische Luftfahrt AG, quickly given the name Swissair.

Swissair made a profit in its first year and, incredibly, it was able to maintain its financial stability throughout almost all of its history, any setbacks suffered having been the result almost exclusively of external factors, such as several oil crises, wars in the Middle East, and currency devaluations. It became known as one of the most prestigious airlines in the world, synonymous with punctuality, reliability and excellent in-flight service, and its sobriquet as The Flying Bank was well deserved.

But throughout its existence, Swissair was handicapped by its small size, which prevented it from providing an effective competition to the larger airlines. It was principally a European niche carrier and only entered the intercontinental market after World War Two. The fact that neutral Switzerland was also outside the European Union affected its access to the market. Swissair came under increasing pressure to follow the trend towards airline alliances, to generate economies of scale to better compete in the global world. Unsuccessful attempts to create a conglomerate that was intended to become a major force in Europe, were followed by surprisingly haphazard partnerships and alliances that brought about Swissair's eventual demise.

It was the acquisition of a large holding in Belgium's national carrier Sabena that led to what became known as the Hunter Strategy, an ambitious, high-risk, and ultimately doomed equity-based alliance programme. The principal aim was to take stakes of between 10 and 25 per cent in smaller European airlines, many already loss-making, with the objective of gaining an overall 20 per cent market share. Extending this alliance building also to the long-haul market was a secondary aspiration. The strategy quickly unravelled. Swissair suffered heavy losses, and neither a strategic re-orientation plan, nor a rescue attempt by the two biggest Swiss banks, failed to arrest its terminal decline. All flights ceased on 2 October 2001 and, although limited operations were resurrected through the winter, guaranteed through a credit line from the government, the last ever flight landed at Zurich on 1 April 2002. Swissair's collapse was seen as a national tragedy, even a humiliation.

Crossair, by far the most profitable of the Sair Group, started operations as SWISS International Air lines, SWISS for short, taking over Swissair's international routes and most aircraft and assets. Now part of Lufthansa, it serves over 100 destinations from Zurich and Geneva. It has come a long way from its air-taxi days as Business Flyers Basle nearly 50 years ago.

Günter Endres

Acknowledgements

The majority of early photos of Swissair and predecessor companies, as well as many others later in the book, have been sourced from the Image Archive of the ETH Library in Zurich. ETH must be congratulated for having digitised a vast collection of photographs, which is freely available. It has been of immense help to me in illustrating this book, and will no doubt be appreciated by other contemporary and future historians.

Swissair, Crossair and Balair have also provided many photographs of their modern fleets, which was much appreciated.

I am also most grateful for the contribution made by Patrick Eberhard, whose superb website, www.sr692.com, is a labour of love and provided much information on background history and the varied fleets of Swissair and predecessors, as well as to Peter Simeon and Aviation History Switzerland on his excellent website, www.swissair00.ch.

As always, there are also many individuals who kindly allowed me to use their photographs to ensure a near complete pictorial coverage. Among these are: Barry Friend Collection, Rudolf Herzog, Gerhard Kammerhuber, Hermann Keist, Hans Versell-Neuhaus, Marcel Tchudin/CRC, John Visanich, Christian Volpati, Maurice Wickstead

My apologies for any inadvertent omissions, and also if I have used some rare photos without express permission. I hope this is accepted with good grace as an important contribution to aviation history.

Haefeli DH-3 '519' on one of its postal flights

Haefeli DH-3 '550' flying over Thun

Swissair and Predecessors

Air transport in Switzerland, a small land-locked country dominated by numerous lakes and the high mountains of the Alps and Jura, had its tentative beginnings not long after the end of World War I. Major Arnold Isler, commander of the military Fliegerabteilung (aviation department) of the Swiss Army, had a vision of aviation that should be developed through a collaboration between military and civil air transport. On 8 January 1919, he set up a trial service for military mail between Zurich/Dübendorf and Berne/Oberlindach, using the Swiss-built Häfeli DH-3, a single-engined, two-seat military reconnaissance biplane. The 63-minute first flight carried military despatches for the General Staff at the Capital Bern, and the aircraft returned to Zurich that same day. On 1 February, he extended the service to Lausanne/La Blécherette, and at the end of April to Geneva, using the DH-3 with serials '51l', '519' and '521', among others. In still conditions, the DH-3 achieved a speed of 120 km, which enabled the Zurich-Geneva link, with the obligatory stops at Lausanne and Bern, to be completed in 2 hours 20 minutes. Encouraged by the qualified technical and operational success achieved, the service was officially inaugurated on a scheduled basis on 1 May, both for the military and the public, at first for mail, small packages and newspapers, but carrying passengers for the first time in June. The single passenger sat in the open observer's seat behind the pilot. After the initial encouraging uptake, traffic declined to such an extent that costs could not be covered. A total of 20,348 pieces of mail and 246 passengers had been carried when the service was suspended on 1 November. Had advertisement been allowed, it may not have been an economic failure. However, by that time, the first commercial companies had already been organised to continue this pioneering work. Isner became the first director of the Eidgenössische Luftamt (Federal Air Office), established on 1 April as a department of Postal Services and Railways, and actively promoted the moves that later led to the founding of Swissair

When the *Fliegerabteilung* underwent drastic cutbacks after the end of the war, many military pilots found themselves redundant and were forced to seek employment in the burgeoning civil sector. One such pilot, Oskar Bider who, between 1 August 1914 and 2 July had completed 4,249 flights, gathered together four of his military colleagues, Ernst Frick, Henri Pillichody, Friedrich Rihner and Balthasar (Balz) Zimmermann, with a view to establishing an air transport company. As a first step, Bider and Rihner set up the *Initiativ-Komité für eine Schweizerische Gesellschaft für Lufttourismus* (Initiative-Committee for a Swiss Airtourism Company), and published a request for financial participations in July 1919. The purpose, as its name suggested, was to provide tourist flights from stations at Zürichhorn, Geneva, Lausanne-Ouchy, Luzerne, Interlaken/Thun, Lugano, Locarno, St Moritz and Rorschach. It was Bider's conviction that with its numerous lakes and large rivers, Switzerland was ideally suited for seaplanes, which would avoid the expensive construction of land-based airport infrastructure. Sadly, Bider died early morning of 7 July, when his Nieuport 23 C1 Bébé fighter stalled and crashed at Dübendorf during an aerial aerobatic display, which he had put on for his military colleagues, to celebrate the completion of his service with the *Fliegerabteilung*. Bider had planned to fly later that same day to Italy to acquire flying-boats for the new airline.

But his plans for a new airline were soon realised as the provisional Frick & Co, Luftverkehrsgesellschaft Ad Astra was founded on 20 September 1919 by the three pilots, Friedrich Rihner, Ernst Frick and Henri Pillichody, laying the groundwork for the establishment of a joint stock company. The prospectus highlighted the progress made during the war in terms of aircraft and pilot training, advantages which should not be lost, adding that the establishment of airports at the most important transport centres would enable the public to participate in flights for business and enjoyment under favourable conditions. It also suggested that the time for the establishment of a Swiss air transport company had never been more favourable, as enthusiasm for flying was growing and ex-military aircraft were available at half their real worth. Emphasis was also placed on the Swiss character of the new undertaking, insisting that in spite of having received much interest for capital and personnel from abroad, the company was to be entirely Swiss.

The official establishment of the Schweizerische Luftverkehrs AG Ad Astra took place on 15 December with a modest capital of CHF (Swiss Francs) 300,000 (then USD 56,950), and flights were operated from Zurichhorn and other locations with a small number of Macchi-Nieuport M.3 and Savoia flying-boats on joyrides from Swiss lakes, completing 104 flights and carrying 251 passengers by the end of the year. But future plans were overtaken by a decision to acquire its competitor Aero-Gesellschaft Comte, Mittelholzer & Co, Luftverlagsanstalt und Passagierflüge, to form a national airline under the name of Schweizerische Luftverkehrs AG Ad Astra Aero. Although that process was completed already on 24 February 1920, yet more changes followed. On 24 April, Avion Tourisme SA was bought and its name added to the company title, making it most unwieldy. However, it was simply referred to as

Alfred Comte, Walter Mittelholzer, Oskar Bider and Henri Pillichody during wartime in 1918

Major Arnold Isler

Friedrich Rihner

Ernst Frick, Emilio Taddeoli and Alfred Comte in front of the Savoia FBA CH-18

Ad Astra. Walter Mittelholzer was appointed chief of the profitable aerial photography department, while Alfred Comte was put in charge of landplanes and was also an enthusiastic aerobatic pilot at air shows. The head office was established at Zurich, with a branch office at Geneva.

Aero-Gesellschaft Comte, Mittelholzer & Co had been founded on 15 April, initially as Aero-Gesellschaft Studer, Mittelholzer & Comte, by Johann Jakob Studer, Walter Mittelholzer and Alfred Comte, as the first commercial air transport company in Switzerland to carry out aerial photography and filming, and joyriding for adventurous passengers over the Alps. The company had its origins in a meeting on 7 January to attract finan-

cial participation to the tune of CHF 50,000 in an enterprise that would serve the Engadin, a long, high Alpine valley in south-eastern Switzerland, renowned for its spectacular scenery. It was suggested that a flight from Zurich would take about an hour and cost would be CHF 400. With Dübendorf reserved for military flying, a home base was eventually found at Schwamendingen-Mattenhof near Zurich, which was opened on 7 May 1919. Flights were begun with a single. two-seat LVG C.V biplane for photography and passenger flights, and a high-wing Kondor E IIIa single-seat parasol monoplane fighter, for aerobatic displays, usually undertaken by Alfred Comte. Both were initially operated without

Ad Astra Aero at Zürichhorn around 1920

markings, except for the Swiss Cross, before being registered CH-2 and CH-1 respectively.

The company was officially registered on 5 November 1919, by which time it had adopted its new title following the departure of Studer. Its fleet had been enlarged with two more LVG C.V, CH-5 and CH-7. By the end of the year, the company had completed 420 flights with around 650 passengers, frequently between Zurich and St Moritz, as well as numerous photography flights. A highlight was the first overflight of the 4,808m high Mont Blanc by Mittelholzer on 11 September.

Avion Tourisme SA was established on 25 June 1919 at Geneva with a capital of CHF 18,000 (USD 5,320) by Maurice Duval, one of the founders of the Swiss Aviation Club, together with industrialist John Gallay, his brother Louis Gallay, and John F Michel. Another key member of the early team was Genevan resident François Durafour, owner of Swiss pilot's licence No.3, who had been offering sightseeing flights from the Saint-Georges shooting range for CHF 50 (USD 9.50) or CHF 100, with his war-surplus Caudron G.3 observation biplane, which he had flown from Paris/Le Bourget to Geneva on

Macchi M.18 CH-21 , M.9bis CH-19 and M.3 CH-15 of Ad Astra Aero and Savoia FBA CH-18 of Avion Tourisme at Lake Lugano. At the rear is a another Savoia. probably S.13 CH-18

LVG C.V biplane CH-2 used for passenger flights and aerial photography

CH-50 was one of two Dornier C.III Komet I high-wing monoplanes operated by Ad Astra Aero

Macchi-Nieuport M.3 CH-15 flown by Walter Mittelholzer

Balair Caudron G.3 biplane CH-146 (Rudolf Herzig)

19 June. Avion Tourisme SA bought the single-engine, two-seat Caudron, which received the Swiss registration CH-3, and concentrated purely on sightseeing flights and joyrides. Technical director and chief pilot was Emilio Taddéoli who, between 1914 and 1919, was a test pilot at the Società Idrovolanti Alta Italia (SIAI) works, later known as Savoia, at Sesto-Calende in Italy. The G.3 was soon joined by the Savoia S.13, CH-4, a two-seat biplane flying-boat powered by a single 187 kW (250 hp) Issotta Fraschini V6 engine. This aircraft was flown to Switzerland by Taddéoli on 12 July 1919 over the Alps, the first crossing of the Alps by a seaplane. While these two aircraft were used for most of the 500 flights undertaken by the end of 1919, the G.3 from Saint-Georges and the flying-boat from Lake Geneva, a further four aircraft, one S.13, CH-6, and three Savoia (FBA) S.13

- CH-14, CH-17 and CH-18 - had been added to the fleet be the end of the year. On 8 December 1919, the company inaugurated a scheduled service over the 60km route between Geneva to Lausanne with CH-14, at a single fare of CHF 75 and CHF 130 return. But with little income during the winter months, Avion Tourisme was unable extricate itself from its financial difficulties. By mid-April 1920, its losses had reached CHF 426,365 (USD 80,950), leading to the take-over by Ad Astra Aero.

To the Stars

Upon its foundation, Ad Astra, had six different types of aircraft, which included two Macchi-Nieuport M.3, three M.9bis and four M.18, four Savoia S.13, three LVG C.V, and one Kondor E IIIa. The Macchi types were all designed by Alessandro Tonini and all were unequal span

Macchi M.9bis eventually registered as CH-19

CH-23 was one of four Macchi M.18 flyingboats which entered service with Ad Astra in 1920

wooden biplane flying-boats of similar size powered by a single Isotta Fraschini engine. The M.3 accommodated two passengers seated side-by-side in an enclosed cabin just forward of the wing, with the pilot in a raised open cockpit further aft. A direct descendant of the M.3, the M.9bis provided seating for four passengers in an enclosed cabin, while the M.18 differed only in detail, with the most notable change having been a more streamlined hull. The S.13 was a two-seat biplane flying-boat, powered by a single 187 kW (250 hp) Isotta Fraschini V6 engine, while the larger S.16 provided space for five passengers and was driven by a more powerful 298 kW (400 hp) Lorraine Dietrich 12Db engine. The two-seat LVG C.V biplane, built by Luft-Verkehrs GmbH in Germany, was powered by a 149 kW (200 hp) Benz Bz IV engine and, together with the Kondor E IIIa single-seat cantilever monoplane, powered by a 149 kW (200 hp) Goebel Goe III engine, was the only landplane in the early fleet.

Claude Dornier himself was on board when a Gs I, a large curious-looking twin-engined all-metal parasol monoplane flying-boat, was delivered to Zurich on 17 October 1919 for trials, which not only proved reliable but also economic. Registered in Switzerland as CH-8, it carried out exploratory flights between Zürichhorn and Lucerne, and was demonstrated at various large towns and cities by Ernst Frick, which proved a great advertisement for the company. Frick, who had a German pilot licence, having worked in Germany during the war as training captain and test pilot, had already carried out trial flights at Dornier during August and September. However, the Gs I was returned to Dornier on 10 December for demonstration flights in the Netherlands and Sweden. But, before the aircraft reached Stockholm, the Allies demanded its destruction, and it was sunk off Kiel on 25 April 1920. The six-passenger Gs I had been intended for a scheduled Geneva-Friedrichshafen service.

The mixed fleet of aircraft, mostly based on World War I reconnaissance types, combined with two accidents at Romanshorn, when Emilio Taddéoli crashed on 24 May 1920 in the Savoia S.13 CH-4 during an

Dornier Gs.I flyingboat CH-8 started operation with Frick & Co in October 1919 but was returned to Dornier in December that year

The BMW VI-powered Dornier Do B Bal Merkur II was widely used in Germany but also found its way to Ad Astra Aero in Switzerland

air show, and Oscar Bereta at Zürichhorn on 31 August that same year in the Savoia S.13 CH-18, with a total of four fatalities, had a negative impact on the balance sheet. As yet, aircraft with their low passenger capacity and their dependence on weather conditions, were no match for railways and other surface transport, and Ad Astra recorded a huge loss of CHF 426,365 in its first year of operation (to October). This, in spite of having completed 4,699 tourist flights with a total of 7,384 passengers, covering 166,920 km in 1,254 hours of flight. The only profitability was achieved from the operations at Zurich (Zürichhorn and Schwamendingen), Geneva and Rohrschach. To ease the situation, the Board of Directors recommended on 23 December 1920 to temporarily reduce operations to Zürichhorn and Geneva, and cut the flight crew to just three pilots, Pillichody, Cartier and Weber.

Of interest was a special flight on 4 March 1920, when Alfred Comte and the famous English stage actor, Robert Bilcliffe Lorraine DSO MC, who had learnt to fly at the Bleriot school at Pau, France, in 1909, took off at St Moritz in the Ad Astra LVG Kondor E IIIa on a flight to London. It proved an eventful journey as fog, snow, engine trouble and three emergency landings ensured frequent delays and the flight took nearly four days. No flights were made between October 1920 and May 1921.

Ad Astra soon started the process of rationalising the fleet with an order for two Dornier C III Komet I four-passenger landplanes, intended for the scheduled 350-km Lindau (Lake Constance)-Geneva service. In the meantime, however, two F 13 were chartered from Junkers for the period June-October 1921, accompanied by pilot Wilhelm Zimmermann. They were given the Swiss registrations CH 59 and CH 66. CH 59 was

The Junkers F 13 CH-66 was initially delivered as a landplane but was soon fitted with floats for initial use from Thunersee (Lake Thun)

Exodus of Kaiser Karl

On 17 October 1921, Hungarian pilot officers Andras Alexay and Ors Fekete, representatives of the Hungarian King (and former Austrian Kaiser) Karl Franz Josef von Habsburg-Lothringen, whose Swiss visa was due to expire a few days later, arrived to make a test flight in one of Ad Astra Aero's aircraft. They had been sent to investigate if the Junkers F 13 was suitable for the King's planned return to Hungary. The aircraft found their approval and Junkers chief pilot Wilhelm Zimmermann, who was temporarily working with the Swiss airline, was selected as pilot, with Captain Fekete joining him in the cockpit. In April 1919, the Austrian Parliament had banished the Habsburgs from Austrian territory unless they renounced all intentions of reclaiming the throne. King Karl and his family moved to Switzerland and had settled down at Chateau de Prangins, near Lake Geneva, in May. Encouraged by Hungarian royalists, his intention was to reclaim the Hungarian crown. Other than in Austria, he had actually never abdicated from his former position in Hungary. His first attempt, travelling to Budapest by train at the end of March 1921, ended in failure, and upon returning to Switzerland, he took up residence at Hertenstein Castle on the shores of Lake Lucerne. From there the royal couple managed to enter Dübendorf airport without arousing the guards' suspicion and immediately after midday on 20 October, F 13 CH 59 took off from Zürich with Zimmermann and Fekete at the controls. In the cabin, Karl and his wife Zita were seated in the rear, while his personal secretary, Aladar von Boroviczeny, and Oberleutnant Andras Alexay, took the front seats. If observed by border guards, it might have been noticed that the aircraft carried two different registration numbers: CH 59 on the fuselage sides and CH 66 on the wings! After a first landing coming up short of the Hungarian border, the aircraft took off again for a five-minute flight and touched down in a field belonging to the legitimist Count Jozsef Cziraky in the village of Denesfa, just on the other side of the Hungarian border, in the disputed territory of Burgenland. Next morning the King was driven to Sopron (Odenburg) and boarded a train bound for Budapest, gathering a force of more than 4,000 loyal volunteers on the way. Eventually, the attempted coup failed because the Regent of the Kingdom of Hungary, Admiral Miklos Horthy, did not support it and refused to step down in favour of the legitimate King because the neighbouring countries threatened

to invade Hungary if Karl was allowed to regain the throne. Karl and Zita were briefly held under Allied guard at Tihany Abbey on Lake Balaton and, in November 1921, were taken to the Danube harbour city of Baja and made to board the British monitor HMS Glowworm. On the Black Sea they were transferred to the light cruiser HMS Cardiff and a few days later arrived in what was to be their final exile, the island of Madeira. Zimmermann returned to Germany, presumably by train, and was banned from entering Switzerland until 1924. The aircraft, which had been paid for by the King, was confiscated by the Hungarian Government. It was put on public display in Budapest by the Magyar Aero Szovetseg (Hungarian Aero Association) on the premises of the national riding school from 22 December 1921 until 10 January 1922. In December 1924 it was formally registered to 'The Property Management of the Royal Family', although the registration mark is not known. It was handed over to the Közlekedesi Muzeum in Budapest, where it has been exhibited ever since - with the wings of CH 66.

equipped with a regular wheeled undercarriage and based at Dübendorf, the airline's main operating base, while CH 66, initially also flown as a landplane from Dübendorf, was soon equipped with floats and first anchored at Thun, then at Zürichhorn. It was with CH 59 that Henri Pillichody set a Swiss height record, when he took the aircraft to 4,331 metres on 18 July, Although Zimmermann had already reached 4,600 metres with CH 66 during a flight on 16 June, this had not been recognised. The F 13, a single-engine all-metal cantilever monoplane for six passengers, was soon to become one of the most prolific aircraft on scheduled services in Europe. Both aircraft were used on sightseeing trips and air-taxi flights. It appears that in the autumn, wings were exchanged between the two aircraft, with CH 59 receiving the larger wings of CH 66. The reasons for this switch remain unclear. However, it is known that CH 59 had sustained damages in a nosing-over.

CH 66 was cancelled from the register on 22 May 1922 and returned to Junkers. CH 59 was earmarked for purchase by Ad Astra after 31 October, but its service was to end in rather dramatic fashion. On 20 October 1921, the former Kaiser (Emperor) of the Austro-Hungarian Empire, Karl Franz Josef von Habsburg-Lothringen, made a second attempt to reclaim the Hungarian crown, which he believed was rightfully his.

Ad Astra was struggling financially and, in spite of carrying 4,027 passengers on 2,254 flights and receiving a subsidy of CHF 200 per month for each pilot who logged at least eight hours on commercial flights, the year 1921 closed with another substantial loss of CH 410,757. Only the photographic department made a profit. The airline began to set its sight on scheduled passenger services and airmail transport and asked Junkers for financial help, which the German manufacturer was keen to provide, as it wanted to develop a southern network and expand

Junkers F 13s CH-92 and CH-94 (below) of Ad Astra Aero were both reregistered in Germany in 1931 and never operated by Swissair

its *Trans-Europa-Union* system. On 16 March 1922, the stock capital of Ad Astra was increased to CFH 400,000 and, in exchange for a 50 per cent shareholding, Junkers agreed to deliver four brand-new F 13 aircraft, together with spare BMW III engines. All four were assembled and test-flown by Zimmermann at Amsterdam, and the first, CH-91, was delivered on 29 May 1922, and on 1 June, Ad Astra director and chief pilot, Henri Pillichody, flew the first commercial air service on the Geneva-Zürich-Nuremberg/Fürth route. The airline received a subsidy of 6,000,000 Reichsmark from Germany and 54,000 francs from the Swiss Government for this service. Ad Astra became part of the *Trans-Europa-Union* on 9 May1923, when the network was further developed. A second F 13 arrived on 30 May and was also registered CH-91 on 28 July to replace the first aircraft with this registration, which, at the request of Junkers, was transferred to Polska Linia Lotnicza Aero-Lloyd in Poland as P-PALA. The reason for the switch is unknown.

The F 13 CH-92 arrived in Switzerland on 24 June 1922, followed by the last two, CH-93 and CH-94 on 6 July. In addition to Pillichody, Ad Astra Aero employed pilots Hans Schaer, Alfred F Leuenberger and later Walter Mittelholzer, who was to become famous as an aviation pioneer. The four aircraft were partly based at Dübendorf, partly at Geneva/Cointrin. Although they were mostly stored, or being repaired during the winter months, Ad Astra occasionally made some flights from the frozen Lake of St Moritz, when fitted with the more powerful BMW IV. Poor load factors, however, resulted in another, albeit reduced, loss of CH 203,768 in 1922. On 14 May 1923, a Geneva-Zurich-Munich link was inaugurated, operated in conjunction with Bayer-

ische Luft-Lloyd, which also used the F 13. At Munich connections were available to Vienna with ÖLAG, and to Nuremberg, Dessau and Berlin by Rumpler Luftverkehr AG. Daily flights were scheduled Mondays to Saturdays. Only 122 paying passengers had been carried in 1922 but the route change brought an improvement to 871 paying passengers in 1923 and a break-even financial performance. Statistics for the year also showed the completion of 1,065 flight hours over 133,000 km, and the carriage of 84 kg of freight and 442 kg of mail.

In 1924, at the request of Aviatik beider Basel, owner of Basle Airport, the F 13s attended the *Mustermesse* (Sample Fair), which took place between 17 and 27 May, and made numerous joyrides, adding more passengers and income. On 20 April, Ad Astra inaugurated a new route from Zurich via Stuttgart to Frankfurt, where connections with other TREU airlines were available to Berlin and Amsterdam. At the same time, the existing Geneava-Zurich-Munich route service was rerouted via Lausanne, and extended to Vienna on 15 May. Walter Mittelholzer took full control over the management of the airline after Alfred Comte had left Ad Astra on 8 December 1920 to found the Alfred Comte, Luftverkehr und Sportfliegerschule, operating six Lohner R flyingboats, CH-60 to CH-65, from Oberrieden. In 1926, he established the Alfred Comte, Schweizerische Flugzeugfabrik, one of whose products, the Comte AC.4 Gentleman, a two-seat braced high-wing monoplane, was acquired by Ad Astra in September 1930, registered CH-262, and used on the Zurich-Lucerne route.

Four Junkers G 24 three-engined all-metal monoplanes were registered to Ad Astra early in 1925 but were never operated. However, how this came

The Swiss-built two-seat Comte AC.4 monoplane CH-262 was briefly used by Ad Astra Aero before forming part of the initial fleet of Swissair

Alfred Comte operated six two-seat Lohner R flyingboats from Oberrieden including CH-62

about is worth recalling. The more powerful aircraft could not be registered in Germany, as it exceeded the limitations imposed on German aviation by the Versailles Peace Treaty. In September 1924, Ad Astra was asked to communicate to the Swiss authorities that Junkers planned to test fly aircraft designated the G 23 to deflect from its true specification, in Switzerland, and at the beginning of January 1925, the second prototype was transported by railway to Dübendorf, where it was assembled. At the same time, Wilhelm Zimmermann applied for a four-week permit to carry out the test flights, but his application was blocked by the Swiss authorities. The reason given was his illegal flight in October 1921 with the former Austrian Kaiser, Karl Franz Josef von Habsburg-Lothringen from Switzerland to Hungary in a Junkers F 13. Zimmermann had resumed flying with the first prototype at Fürth on 23 December 1924 and in January familiarisation flights had been made with two

other Junkers company pilots, Waldemar Roeder and Paul Witte. It was possibly Witte who took Zimmermann's place at Dübendorf, when the second prototype flew for the first time on 2 February. It was registered as CH-132, with one Junkers L 2 and two Mercedes D IIIs and received a Certificate of Airworthiness on 2 March. Test flights revealed no significant problems and it was approved for a crew of two and up to ten passengers. CH-133 was the first G 24 with three Junkers L 2, and this aircraft, named *Sachsen*, together with CH-134 *Österreich* and CH-135 *Bayern*, were owned and operated by the Bayerische Luftverkehrs AG on the network of the *Trans-Europa-Union*. Several other types of aircraft from Junkers and Dornier were registered to Ad Astra to circumvent the Inter-Allied Aeronautical Commission of Control (IAACC).

The three-engine Junkers G 23 CH-133 was registered in Switzerland to obviate post-war restrictions on German aircraft but was never used

Aircraft registered to Ad Astra Aero but never used

CH-66	Junkers F 13	581
CH-87	Dornier Do H Falke	
CH-126	Dornier Do C	52/62
CH-127	Dornier Do E	58 or 9
CH-128	Junkers S 22 (J 22)	408
CH-129	Junkers H 21	801
CH-130	Junkers A 20	821
CH-132	Junkers G 24	832
CH-133	Junkers G 24	834
CH-134	Junkers G 24	839
CH-135	Junkers G 24	848

German influence removed

For political reasons, Ad Astra Aero could not open a service from Basle in the direction of Frankfurt, as the Allies had prohibited flights across the western banks of the River Rhine. As a result, Zürich grew to become the main airport for services to and from Switzerland. Only later, in April 1924, did it become possible to open a service to Frankfurt via Stuttgart, but then only for freight and mail. Ad Astra was forced to leave TREU in early 1925, as the Swiss authorities had deemed that the airline was an international company and would, therefore, no longer provide much-needed subsidies. However, it retained a RM 3,000 interest

and became one of eighteen members of the enlarged *Europa-Union KGA*, which was established on 7 May 1925. It never became an operational member, and by the time a capital increase was on the table the following September, it had left the union, citing political difficulties. All German influence was now removed.

New routes included Zurich-Stuttgart, where a connection to Hamburg was available, opened on 12 April 1926, followed on 3 May, linking Geneva with Lausanne and Zurich. Both services operated until 30 September and the results were more than satisfactory, Ad Astra recording 784 flights, 269,930 km flown, 1,389 passengers, 11,894 kg of mail, 861 kg of freight and 2,898 kg excess baggage. In addition to its scheduled services, the airline also continued to carry out aerial photography, joyrides and aerial surveys. Some special flights were performed with the F 13 including a seven-hour trip with passengers from Basle to Naples on 21 May 1926. Flown by Walter Mittelholzer, the aircraft returned to Zurich three days later. In the meantime, the fleet had been boosted by the two six-passenger Dornier Do B Bal Merkur II, CH-142 and CH-171. On 24 June, Mittelholzer, with co-pilot Zinsmair, set up three world records in CH-171 for duration, distance covered, and speed, carrying 500 kg, and followed up with four more records with a useful load of 1,000 kg. On 11 April 1930, Ad Astra added a single high-wing BFW/Messerschmitt M 18d, CH-191, powered by an Armstrong Lynx engine and with accommodation for four passengers.

CH-155 was one of five Fokker-Grulich F.III operated, seen here being loaded with cargo at Basle

The network was unchanged in 1927, but the following year, Ad Astra handed the Geneva-Zurich-Munich service to new Swiss competitor Balair, inaugurating in its place a Munich link from Basle via Zurich, which became the first year-round international service to be flown by a Swiss airline. Another domestic service was started between Lausanne, Biel and Zurich, flown in co-operation with Balair. Ad Astra, in pool with Deutsche Luft Hansa, also opened an express service between Zurich and Berlin, flown by the new Dornier Merkur, and another between Zurich, Stuttgart and Frankfurt a/Main. The 680-km Zurich-Berlin service was then the longest non-stop route in Europe and took some five hours. A decision by the Swiss Federal Air Agency in 1929 that all international services were to be flown with multi-engined aircraft for safety reasons, resulted in the introduction of the Fokker F.VIIb-3m and hastened the withdrawal of the F 13. One aircraft, CH 93, had already been written-off after an emergency landing near Frankfurt on 14 June 1928 during which the pilot, F Chardon and three passengers were seriously injured.

Balz Zimmermann who played a leading part in early Swiss air transport

Ad Astra took delivery of its three Armstrong-Siddeley Lynx-powered Fokker F.VIIb-3m, CH-190, CH-192 and CH-193, in 1929/30, which represented a significant modernisation of its fleet. The wooden Fokker Trimotor as it became known, was one of the most significant commercial airliners of the inter-war years, not only forming the main fleets of a number of European and American airlines, but also becoming the aircraft of choice for many experimental long-distance flights. The high-wing aircraft normally provided accommodation for two crew and eight passengers.

Competition and co-operation

The Basler Luftverkehrs-Aktiengesellschaft had been founded by Dr Alphonse Ehinger, who became president, Paul Joerin, Dr Robert Labhardt, Friedrich Schwarz and Dr Rudolf Speich on 4 September 1925, with a modest capital of CHF 100,000 (USD 19,325). The establishment of the airline was a direct result of a planned service by the German regional airline Badish-Pfälzische Luftverkehrsgesellschaft from Frankfurt to Basle via Mannheim. Karlsruhe, Baden-Baden and Freiburg. However, as the German airline was not allowed to fly over the 50km-wide demilitarised zone along the River Rhine, the importance of such a service was recognised by the wealthy business community in the third-largest Swiss city.

Operations started with a service from Basle/Sternen-feld-Birsfelden to Freiburg/Breisgau and Mannheim with a single German-built Fokker-Grulich F.IIb, registered CH-151, which was formerly operated by the German airline as D 175 and was flown by the Swiss company's then only pilot, the German Otto Rahn. On 1 April 1926, the name of the company was changed slightly to Basler Luftverkehrs AG, abbreviated to Balair, reflecting the French name for Basle, Bâle. Balz Zimmerman, who later became a founding member of Swissair, took on the role of managing director. Throughout its short history, Balair relied entirely on high-wing wooden Fokker aircraft, progressively improving the fleet, first with five ex-KLM Fokker-Grulich F.III, CH-152 to CH-156, which formed the backbone of the fleet in the early years. The five F.IIIs were flown in formation from Amsterdam/Schiphol to Basle on 10 April 1926 by KLM pilots Gerrit Geysendorffer, John Scholte, Leendert Sillevis, Jan Duimelaar and Iwan Smirnoff.

The F.II, powered by the 138 kW (185 hp) BMW IIIa water-cooled engine, had accommodation for four passengers in an enclosed cabin under the wings, while the five, newly-built F.III were larger aircraft with a wider fuselage to accommodate five passengers. CH-156 crashed during an emergency landing on approach to Nyon, Switzerland already on 1 May 1926, and CH-153 was lost in an accident at Blécherette, near Lausanne in 1927. CH-155 was sold to a new Swiss airline, Ostschweizerische Aero-Gesellschaft St Gallen, on 1 August 1927. The remaining two aircraft, CH-152 and CH-154 were sold to Italian airline. Aviolinee Italiane SA (ALI)

Walter Mittelholzer – pilot and pioneer photographer

Couzy, Dr Heim, Mittelholzer and Hartmann before leaving for Africa

Born in St Gallen on 2 April 1984, Walter Mittelholzer trained as a photographer, and at the outbreak of the First World War volunteered as a spotter for the fledgling air force, obtaining his pilot's licence in 1917. He became a director and chief pilot of Ad Astra Aero, and technical director of Swissair upon its foundation in 1931. But his fame derived not from his managerial prowess, but from his daring local and international flying expeditions, where he used his skills as a pilot, photographer and film-maker to record a previously unseen exotic world in flight and on the ground. His first adventure found him at Spitsbergen, where an intended relief operation for the Amundsen North Pole attempt was turned into an aerial reconnaissance mission. The Junkers F 13 D-260 Eisvogel, piloted by Arthur Neumann, made three flights between 6 and 8 July 1923, covering a total distance of 1.700 km and generating aerial photographs never seen before. But his most famous flight began on 7 December 1926, when he, accompanied by pilot mechanic Hans Hartmann, Swiss geologist Dr Arnold Heim, and geographer René Couzy, left Zurich in the float-equipped Dornier Merkur CH-171, named Switzerland for the occasion, left for Africa to study the geography and geology of the region from Egypt to the African lakes. Space was provided for the photographic records and there was a dark room for developing films; the cabin could also be used as a sleeping place when the machine was in an isolated location. The low petrol consumption of the 335/447 kW (450/600 hp) BMW VI engine, with its reserve of power and a cruising speed of 150 km/h, and the excellence of the all-metal construction, contributed to the success of the trip.

Mittelholzer took off from Zurich and flew to Cairo via Pisa, Naples, Athens and Abu Qir. Continuing on to Luxor and Aswan, Khartoum, Malakal, Mongalla, Butiaba on Lake Albert, and Jinja on Lake Victoria. A necessary engine repair kept them at Jinja from 8-30 January. Flights were also made to Kisumu, Mwanza, Bukoba, other places around Lake Tanganyika. The two scientists left in Rhodesia, after which Mittelholzer and Hartmann made a tour of East and Southern Africa, landing at Cape Town on 21 February 1927, having covered over 20,000 km in little more than 100 flying hours. Aircraft and crew made the journey home by steamship. On 8 January 1930, with Alfred Künzle as second pilot and Werner Wegmann as mechanic, Mittelholzer crossed the 5,895 m high Mount Kilimanjaro, having taken the banker Baron Louis de Rothschild on a big game hunting trip to the Serengeti Plain in the Fokker F.VIIb-3m CH-190. The

trip took place from 15 December 1929 to 28 February 1930. Like the Kilimanjaro flight, the Lake Chad flight was a tourist expedition funded by the client, this time the American businessman and adventurer Kingsley Macomber. That flight, with Franz Zimmermann as co-pilot, also in CH-190, left Zurich on 2 December 1930 and took the travel party over Spain, Morocco and the Atlas Mountains to the Sahara Desert. The flightpath then continued over the Niger to Senegal, before heading northwards again to the African coasanut, back over Spain and France, arriving home on 23 Jan. 1931. Plans to fly over Everest did not materialise.In the meantime, he had flown a Junkers A 20, also named Switzerland, to Tehran under contract to Junkers to demonstrate the aircraft to the Persian authorities. He had left Zurich on 18 December 1924, and had arrived in the Persian capital on 27 January 1925, having been held up in Turkey for a month due to diplomatic problems. Between 17 February 1928 and 6 March 1929, he had also made a trip around the Western Mediterranean in Junkers F 13 CH-94, taking many aerial photographs. He embarked on what turned out to be his final long-distance venture on 2 February 1934, when he took off from Zurich in the Swissair Fokker F.VIIb-3m CH-192, which he was to deliver to the Abyssinian Emperor Haile Selassie. Facing danger to the last, he died in a climbing accident on the Stangenwand in the Hochschwab massif in Austria on 9 May 1937. In his short life, he completed more than 9,000 flights and taken well over 100,000 photographs.

Walter Mittelholzer's Fokker F.VIIb-3m CH-190 on Kilimanjaro flight

Junkers A 20 CH-130 at Busheer on the way to demonstrating the aircraft to the Persian authorities

Balair Fokker F.IIb CH-151 after pilot Ulrich Keller was forced into an emergency landing near Cossonay

in January 1929. Ostschweizerische Aero-Gesellschaft St Gallen was founded on 25 July 1927 to provide sight-seeing flights over Lake Constance and the Säntis in the Appenzell Alps, but by 1929 had progressed to daily feeder services from St Gallen/Breitenfeld to Dübendorf and Basle, where connections were available to international destinations. These were flown with a single-engine Hopfner HV.628 high-wing strut-braced mono-plane with accommodation for up to six passenger. The only example built, CH-186, was delivered to St Gallen on 19 April 1929 and used until scrapped two years later.

Balair quickly built up a small but effective route system that provided good connections to major European capitals. A connection was introduced on 12 April 1926 to Stuttgart, where passengers could transfer to Berlin. A Basle-Karlsruhe-Frankfurt service was added a week later, jointly with Deutsche Luft Hansa, which provided connections to Amsterdam, Hamburg and Copenhagen. This was followed by a trial service over the 80km route from Basle to Zurich, which operated from 19 April to 3 May and provided a connection to Munich and Vienna. Another short route, also of only 80km, was

Balair Fokker F.II CH-152 and Fokker F.VIIa CH-158 at Basle-Birsfelden

Fokker V.IIa CH-157 on the iced-over Moritzsee (Lake Moritz)

opened between Basle and La Chaux-de-Fonds on 17 May and operated until 30 September. A Basle-Geneva-Lyon route was added on 24 May with a connecting flight by French airline Air Union to Marseille, where steamers left with mail for the Orient. Aviatik beider Basel, operator of the Basle airport, provided a bus service to and from Berne, which picked up passengers one hour after arrival of a Balair flight for Berne, and delivered passengers one hour before the flight to Basle. Operations were sustained with subsidies from the government and the Swiss Post, Telegraph and Telephones (PTT) agency. In its first year, the fast-growing airline operated 1,568 scheduled flights carrying 903 passengers, 8,398 kg of mail, 1,308 kg of goods, and 2,540 kg of excess baggage. The largest amount of mail was transported on the Lyon service for onward flights to Marseille.

Balair entered into a co-operative agreement with Dutch airline KLM on the Amsterdam route, which was jointly inaugurated on 2 May 1927 from Zurich via Basle, Brussels and Rotterdam. That same year, the Basle-La Chaux-de-Fonds service was extended to Lausanne with the support of the City of Lausanne on the shores of Lake Geneva. Other domestic services were added from Lausanne to Zurich via Biel and from Basle to St Gallen, both flown in co=operation with Ad Astra Aero. The improvement of the fleet continued with the acquisition of the eight-passenger, single-engined Fokker

F.VIIa, the first of which, CH-157, entered service on 28 March 1927, followed by two more, CH-158 and CH-159, in March 1928. All three were acquired at a unit cost of CHF 90,000. After the delivery of the last two F.VIIas, Balair took over the Geneva-Zurich-Munich-Vienna service from Ad Astra Aero. At the same time, the Amsterdam service was rerouted over Germany, now taking in Mannheim, Frankfurt, Dusseldorf, Essen/Muhlheim and Rotterdam, also flown jointly with KLM.

The Swiss Authorities made it known that if Balair and Ad Astra Aero were to continue to operate international services, new three-engined aircraft were to be used to qualify for the continued subsidy. As a result, therefore, 1929 saw a great change in the fleet structure of Balair. The obsolete Fokker-Grulich F.IIb, CH-151, was broken up and cancelled from the register. In January 1929, Balair managed to sell two Fokker F.IIIs (CH-152 and CH-154) to the Italian airline company Aviolinee Italiane SA (ALI). The first Fokker F.VIIb-3m, CH-160, was delivered in April 1929, but only remained part of the fleet until August when it was sold to CLASSA in Spain as M-CAHH. At the end of the flying-season of 1929, Balair sold two of its Fokker F.VIIas to the Danish airline company DDL, where they received the registration OY-DED and OY-DAD. By 1 February 1930 Balair owned just one Fokker F.VIIa, CH-157. The remaining aircraft had been sold or lost in accidents.

Balair's fourth three-engine Fokker F.VIIb-3m CH-165, which formed part of the early Swissair fleet

In 1929 the company had already reduced its network considerably, mainly due to lack of aircraft, but also as a result of the Great Depression, which depressed demand for air travel. Only international services to Amsterdam, Vienna and Marseille were flown in co-operation with both KLM and Deutsche Luft Hansa. The service to Marseille no longer made a stopover in Lyon, but now there was a direct flight between Geneva and Marseille. The domestic services were taken over by Ad Astra Aero. In February 1930 the first of four new aircraft to be delivered that year arrived at Balair's base. The Fokker F.VIIb-3m was registered CH-161 on 17 February. but only served until 30 October of that year, as it crashed that day on approach to a foggy Essen/Mülheim, Germany, and was damaged beyond repair. There were no casualties. In March 1930, a batch of three new Fokker F.VIIb-3m arrived from Amsterdam (CH-162 to CH-164), which all went to Swissair in March 1931, as did another, CH-165, which was registered on 28 February 1931.

In 1930 Balair lost its pool partner to Amsterdam (KLM), as the Dutch company started up its service to the Far East and needed all the material and efforts to be put into this, a vital service for the Netherlands. The route from Geneva to Basle, Mannheim, Frankfurt am Main, Cologne, and Essen/Mülheim to Amsterdam was

now operated in pool with Lufthansa. Domestic services, Basle-St Gallen- Zurich and Basle-Lucerne, could once again be opened. The service from Vienna to Munich and Zurich continued to Geneva as well, thus creating another domestic service. An interesting airmail route was operated from Basle to Cherbourg and Le Havre in a joint effort between Balair and French airline Air Union SA, to deliver mail to the steamers that left these two French coastal cities for the United States each week. In these two French harbour cities the mail steamers for the USA left every week. An average of 500kg of mail was transported on the weekly flight. Balair initially used its single F.VIIa, while awaiting delivery of its new three-engined F.VIIb-3ms.

But Balair was still struggling to survive and was not aided by the Swiss Government, which cut subsidies by 10 per cent, a situation Ad Astra also found itself in. It was a thinly-disguised move by the authorities to force a merger between the two loss-making airlines. A general assembly by Ad Astra on 17 March 1931 agreed the dissolution of the airline backdated to 31 December. Balair followed suit and the two airlines were merged on 26 March 1931, retroactive from 1 January, to form Swissair.

Ad Astra Aero Fleet 1920-1931

Macchi-Nieuport M.3 (2)

Two-passenger unequal span biplane flying-boat, powered by a single 118 kW (160 hp) Isotta-Fraschini V.4B water-cooled inline engine, generating a cruising speed of 127 km/h (79 mph)

CH-12		24.02.20-16.01.22	ex Frick & Co; burnt out
CH-15	3022	24.02.20-21.11.21	ex Frick & Co; broken up

Macchi-Nieuport M.9bis (2)

Four-passenger unequal span biplane flying-boat, powered by a single 186 kW (250 hp) Isotta-Fraschini V.6 water-colled inline engine, generating a crusing speed of 160 km/h (100 mph)

CH-19	3049	24.02.20-12.10.23	ex Frick & Co; damaged beyond repair
CH-20		24.02.20-02.02.23	ex Frick & Co; burnt out

Macchi-Nieuport M.18 (4)

Three-passenger unequal span biplane flying-boat, powered by a single 186 kW (250 hp) Isotta-Fraschini V.6 water-cooled inline engine, generating a cruising speed of 145 km/h (90 mph)

CH-21	24.02.20-00.00.22	to Junkers
Ch-22	24.02.20-	
CH-23	24.02.20-00.00.22	to Junkers
CH-24	24.02.20-	

Caudron G.3 (1)

Single-seat sesquiplane, powered by one Le Rhône 9C air-cooled piston engine, generating a maximum speed of 106 km/h (66 mph)

CH-3	21.04.20	ex Avion Tourisme but not used

Kondor E.IIIa (1)

Single-seat parasol monoplane, powered by one 149 kW (200 hp) Goebel Goe III air-cooled piston engine, generating a mazimum speed of 190 km/h (120 mph)

CH-1	24.02.20-	ex Aero-Gesellschaft Comte, Mittelholzer & Co

LVG C.V (5)

Two-seat wire-braced biplane, powered by a single 150 kW (200 hp) Benz Bz IV engine, generating a cruising speed of 164 km/h (102 mph)

CH-2	24.02.20-00.00.27	ex Aero-Gesellschaft Comte, Mittelholzer & Co; to Deutsche Luft Hansa
CH-5	24.02.20-	
CH-7	24.02.20-00.00.22	ex Aero-Gesellschaft Comte, Mittelholzer & Co, wfu
CH-75	00.05.22-	
CH-76	00.05.22-	

Savoia S.13 FBA (1)

Two-seat two-bay biplane flying-boat, powered by a single 186 kW (250 hp) Isotta-Fraschini 200 wayer-cooled engine, generating a maximum speed of 243 km/h (151 mph)

CH-6	7195	21.04.20-12.11.24	ex Avion Tourisme; probably sold to France
CH-14		21.04.20-30.04.21	ex Avion Tourisme; broken up
CH-17		21.04.20-10.05.22	exAvion Tourisme; broken up
CH-18		24.02.20-31.08.20	ex Avion Tourisme; crashed on completion of a demonstration flight into the lake off Zürichhorn, killing the pilot Oscar Bereta

Savoia S.16 (1)

Five-seat two-bay biplane flying-boat, powered by a single 186 kW (250 hp) Isotta-Fraschini V.6 water-cooled inline engine, generating a maximum speed of 197 km/h (122 mph)

CH-4		21.04.20-24.05.20	ex Ad Astra; crashed at Romanshorn, Thurgau, after wing structural failure, killing the pilot Emilio Taddeoli

Dornier Do C III Komet I (1)

Four-passenger high-wing braced monoplane, powered by a single 138 kW (185 hp) BMW IIIa engine, generating a cruising speed of 130 km/h (81 mph)

CH-49	22	11.02.21-16.02.21	returned to Dornier

Dornier Do P Bal Komet II (1)

Four-passenger high-wing braced monoplane, powered by a single 186 kW (250 hp) BMW IV engine, generating a cruising speed of 135 km/h (84 mph)

CH-50	*2/23	02.07.21-12.05.22	returned to Germany

Dornier Do L 2 Delphin II (1)

Four-passenger high-wing monoplane flying-boat, powered by a single 186 kW (250 hp) BMW IV engine, generating a cruising speed of 125 km/h (78 mph)

CH-58		00.00.21-00.00.22	wfu

Junkers F 13 (7)

Six-passenger all-metal monoplane, powered by a single 136 KW (185 hp) BMW IIIa engine, generating a maximum speed of 170 km/h (105 mph)

CH-59	574	01.06.21-20.10.21	interned in Hungary; aircraft had wings of CH-66
CH-66	581	23.06.21-12.05.22	leased from and returned to Junkers and reregistered as D 203, named Bussard
CH-91(1)	580	29.05.22-28.07.22	returned to Junkers
CH-91 (2)	583	30.05.22-20.10.31	cancelled from Swiss Air Register
CH-92	587	24.06.22-31.12.30	to Fliegerhorst Nordmark GmbH, Germany
CH-93	593	06.07.22-14.06.28	destroyed after emergency landing at Frankfurt am Main, Germany
CH-94	617	06.07.22-26.03.31	to Swissair

Wild WT/WT-S (3)

Two-seat strut-braced biplane, powered by a single 89 kW (120 hp) Argus As-II water-cooled inline engine, generating a maximum speed of 145 km/h (90 mph)

CH-71	13	25.10.21-18.09.21	ex Swiss Air Force '141'; crashed at Mezieres on flight from Solothurn to Lausanne, killing both occupants
CH-74	54	00.00.21-24.09.30	ex Swiss Air Force '152'; written off
CH-122	18	00.00.24-	ex Swiss Air Force '146'; sold to Germany

Hanriot HD-1 (1)

Single-seat strut-braced biplane, powered by one 81 kW (109 hp) Le Rhône 9J air-cooled piston engine, generating a maximum speed of 184 km/h (114 mph)

CH-77		00.00.21-29.03.22	crashed at Guldenstock, Tödi. Pilot Walter Mittelholzer the sole occuant was injured

Dornier Do B Bal Merkur II (2)

Eight-passenger high-wing monoplane, powered by a single 450 kW (600 hp) BMW VI water-cooled engine, generating a cruising speed of180 km/h (110 mph)

CH-142	77	20.05.27-26.03.31	to Swissair
CH-171	165	08.10.26-26.03.31	to Swissair

Haefeli DH-3 (1)

Two-seat strut-braced biplane, powered by a single 89 kW (120 hp) Argus As II water-cooled inline engine, generating a maximum speed of 145 km/h (90 mph)

Fokker F.VIIb-3 (3)

10-passenger high-wing cantilever monoplane, powered by three 150 kW (200 hp) Armstrong Siddeley Lynx Mk.IV engines, generating a crusing speed of 190 km/h (118 mph)

CH-190	5128	28.02.29-26.03.31	to Swissair
CH-192	5225	01.05.30-26.03.31	to Swissair
CH-193	5136	29.08.30-26.03.31	to Swissair

BFW/Messerschmitt M 18 d (1)

Four-passenger cantilever shoulder-wing monoplane, powered by a 171 KW (230 hp) Armstrong Siddeley Lynx engine, generating a cruising speed of 140 km/h (87 mph)

CH-191	478	11.04.30-26.03.31	to Swissair

Comte AC-4 Gentleman (1)

Two-passenger strut-braced high-wing monoplane, powered by a 78 kW (105 hp) Cirrus Hermes III engine, generating a cruising speed of 140 km/h (87 mph)

CH-262	34	18.09.30-26.03.31	to Swissair

Balair Fleet 1925-1931

Fokker-Grulich F.IIb (1)

Four-passenger high-wing monoplane, powered by a single 136 kW (185 hp) BMW IIIa engine, generating a cruising speed of 120 km/h (74.5 mph)

CH-151	1503	00.00.25-00.00.29	ex Badish-Pfälzische Luftfahrtgesellschaft D-175; boken up

Fokker-Grulich F.III (5)

Five-passenger high-wing monoplane, powered by a 179 kW (240 hp) Armstrong Siddeley Puma water-cooled inline engine, generating a cruising speed of 135 km/h (84 mph)

CH-152	1503	10.04.26-19.01.29	ex KLM H-NABG; sold to Aviolinee Italiane (ALI), later registered as I-AANJ
CH-153	1506	10.04.26-00.00.27	ex KLM H-NABJ; crashed at Blecherette near Lausanne
CH-154	1507	10.04.26-19.01.29	ex KLM H-NABK; sold to Aviolinee Italiane (ALI), later registered as I-AANK
CH-155	1510	10.04.26-01.08.27	ex KLM H-NABN; sold to Aero-St Gallen
CH-156	1529	10.04.26-01.05.26	ex KLM H-NABQ; crashed during an emergency landing on approach to Nyon

Fokker F.VIIa (3)

Eight-passenger high-wing monoplane, powered by a single 298 kW (400 hp) Gnome Rhône Jupiter air-cooled radian engine, generating a cruising speed of 155 km/h (96 mph)

CH-157	5005	28.03.27-26.03.31	to Swissair
CH-158	5053	00.03.28-00.00.29	sold to DDL as OY-DAD
CH-159	5054	00.03.28-00.00.29	sold to DDL as OY-DED

Fokker F.VIIb-3m (6)

10-passenger high-wing cantilever monoplane, powered by three 150 kW (200 hp) Armstrong Siddeley Lynx Mk.IV engines, generating a crusing speed of 190 km/h (118 mph)

CH-160	5127	00.04.29-00.08.29	sold to CLASSA as M-CAHH
CH-161	5207	17.02.30-30.10.30	crashed on approach to Essen/Mülheim, Germany
CH-162	5208	11.03.30-26.03.31	to Swissair
CH-164	5209	11.03.30-26.03.31	to Swissair
CH-165	5195	11.03.30-26.03.31	to Swissair
CH-166	5238	28.02.31-26.03.31	to Swissair

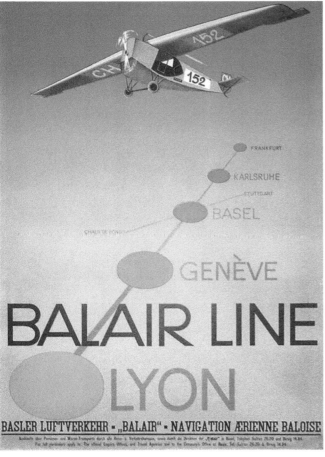

Swissair Geneaology

Frick & Co Luftverkehrsgesellschaft Ad Astra
20 September 1919 ⟶ Schweizerische Luftverkehrs AG Ad Astra
15 December 1919

Aero-Gesellschaft Studer, Mittelholzer & Comte
15 April 1919

Aero-Gesellschaft Comte, Mittelholzer & Co
5 November 1919 ⟶ Schweizerische Luftverkehrs AG Ad Astra Aero
24 February 1920

Avion Tourisme SA
25 June 1919 ⟶ Schweizerische Luftverkehrs AG Ad Astra Aero,
Avion Tourisme (Ad Astra Aero)
21 April 1920

Basler Luftverkehrs-Aktiengesellschaft
4 September 1925

Basler Luftverkehrs AG (Balair)
1 April 1926 ⟶ **Swissair** ⟵
(Scheizerische Luftverkehr AG)
26 March 1931 (1 January 1931)

Passengers being checked-in at Zurich

Swissair

Although Switzerland was spared the direct impact of the First World War, its dependency on exports and imports was severely exposed in the Great Depression, which began in the United States with the Wall Street Crash on 24 October 1929, and rapidly spread throughout Europe and elsewhere. With the confidence in the future severely dented, governments and companies were forced to cut back on spending. The aviation sector was not immune from this downturn. On 30 March 1930, the Swiss Government cut its subsidies by 10 per cent, based on 600,000 km flown annually on the main routes, in the full knowledge that the airlines would struggle to remain afloat with the reduced income from the State, having already experienced a worrying decrease in demand. The government move was seen as a gentle nudge towards consolidation, which took place on 26 March 1931, when Ad Astra Aero and Balair, which had already co-operated closely, merged to form the Schweizerische Luftverkehr AG, made retroactive from 1 January

After initial resistance from members of the Federal Council, the name Swissair was chosen for the new airline. It had been proposed by Dr Alphonse Ehinger, president of the management board of Balair. Swissair disposed of a capital of CHF 800,000 (USD 155,200), which was provided by Balair (CHF 500,000) and Ad Astra (CHF 300,000) and was headed by Balz Zimmermann and Walter Mittelholzer and started its new existence with 64 personnel, among them 10 pilots, seven radio operators and eight flight engineers, and 13 aircraft with a total capacity of 85 passengers. Its international network included six routes, Geneva-Zurich-Munich-Vienna, Geneva-Basle-Mannheim-Frankfurt-Cologne-Essen-Amsterdam,and Berne-Zurich-Stuttgart-Leipzig/Halle-Berlin, operated in conjunction with Deutsche Luft Hansa; Zurich-Basle-Paris, jointly with CIDNA; Geneva-Lyon-Paris with Air Union; and Basle-Zurich-Nuremberg-Prague. A domestic Zurich-Luzern route was also flown, as was an airmail route from Basle to Cherbourg/Le Havre with CIDNA and Air Union, to meet the transatlantic steamships, all adding up

to a network of 4,203 km. Operations were maintained between 1 March and 31 October, although the Prague and Paris-Lyon services terminated on 30 September each year, and the Zurich-Luzern route was operated only between 15 June and 20 September. Its flight programme also included numerous Alpine sightseeing flights. In its first year, Swissair flew 724,476 km and carried 10,282 passengers, and 254,936 kg of mail and freight. Of the passenger total, 2,619 were transported on special flights and sightseeing services. Swissair recorded a net profit of CHF 49,453 in the year, enabling it to pay a 4 per cent dividend of CFH 20 per share. Incredibly, its financial stability was maintained through the next 68 years of its history, with Swissair achieving regular profitability, with few exceptions, which later gained it the nickname of *The Flying Bank*.

The two Dornier Merkur aircraft were never used by Swissair and were later scrapped, and the BFW/Messerschmitt M 18 d, reregistered HB-IME on 1 October 1934, was used until sold to the Farner Works at Grenchen on 25 January 1938. The Comte AC-4 had the longest

ex-Balair Fokker F.VIIa CH-157 at a frozen St Moritz now with Swissair titles

The ex-Balair Fokker F.VIIb-3 CH-166

life with the airline. Operated primarily on the Zurich-Lucerne feeder route and the Basle-Zurich sector of the express service to Vienna, it was provided with a better engine in 1933 and was reregistered HB-IKO. It was sold to a private owner in November 1947. The mainstay of the early fleet thus were the three Fokker F.VIIb-3m acquired from Ad Astra, although their record was not exemplary. HB-LAK, the former CH-190, crash-landed at Promasens, Switzerland, on 12 April 1935 and was cannibalised for spares, and CH-193 had been inexplicably destroyed by fire during refuelling at Paris/Le Bourget on 19 June 1931. CH-192 was sold to Emperor Haile Selassie I of Ethiopia. All five ex-Balair, Wright Whirlwind-powered aircraft were sold to Italy's Ala Littoria in the summer of 1935, following the introduction of more modern aircraft. The only single-engine Fokker F.VIIa, CH-157/HB-LBO, powered by the Bristol Jupiter, was re-engined with the Wright Cyclone, which improved performance on the Basle-Cherbourg/Le Havre service. In 1939, it had its passenger capacity increased from eight to 10. It was then removed from regular passenger service and used for training and sightseeing flights until 1950. It has been displayed in the *Verkehrshaus* (Transport Museum) at Lucerne since 1972.

On 16 July 1932, the new civil area at Dübendorf was opened to traffic and included a terminal, a hangar for two aircraft, a maintenance workshop and a hangar for general aviation. Two-thirds of the area was now taken up by the military, and one-third by civil activities, with both under separate management. The new civil facilities provided not only security but also facilitated the expansion of flights. On 1 May 1933, Swissair opened its first Transalpine route with a service from Zurich to Milan, in co-operation with Avio Linee Italiane (ALI), and on the same day also added a Zurich-Basle-Frankfurt schedule. On the same day in 1934, it added Geneva-Bern-Zurich and Basle-Zurich routes to feed into the Zurich-Vienna and Zurich-Berlin services. Between 1 May and 31 August that year, Swissair flew a Basle-Frankfurt night postal and cargo service, which linked into the European night airmail network at Frankfurt. It became an all-year service in 1938.

Swissair Founding Fleet 1931

CH-142	Dornier Do B Bal Merkur	2 x BMW VI	ex Ad Astra
CH-157	Fokker F.VIIa	1 x Bristol Jupiter	ex Balair
CH-162	Fokker F.VIIb-3m	3 x Wright Whirlwind	ex Balair
CH-163	Fokker F.VIIb-3m	3 x Wright Whirlwind	ex Balair
CH-164	Fokker F.VIIb-3m	3 x Wright Whirlwind	ex Balair
CH-165	Fokker F.VIIb-3m	3 x Wright Whirlwind	ex Balair
CH-166	Fokker F.VIIb-3m	3 x Wright Whirlwind	ex Balair
CH-171	Dornier Do B Bal Merkur	2 x BMW VI	ex Ad Astra
CH-190	Fokker F.VIIb-3m	3 x Armstrong-Siddeley Lynx	ex Ad Astra
CH-191	BFW/Messerschmitt M 18 d	1 x Armstrong-Siddeley Lynx	ex Ad Astra
CH-192	Fokker F.VIIb-3m	3 x Armstrong-Siddeley Lynx	ex Ad Astra
CH-193	Fokker F.VIIb-3m	3 x Armstrong-Siddeley Lynx	ex Ad Astra
CH-262	Comte AC-4 Gentleman	1 x Cirrus Hermes	ex Ad Astra

The only single-engine Fokker operated was this F.VIIa HB-LBO, previously CH-157

HB-LAN was one of five ex-Balair Fokker F.VIIb-3m sold to Ala Littoria in Italy in summer 1935

The only Swiss-built aircraft in the early fleet, the Comte AC-4 Gentleman CH-262, here advertising Eglisana mineral water, was operated until November 1947

The BFW/Messerschmitt M 18 CH-191 had an accident at Basle-Sternefeld on 2 May 1932 but was repaired and served until 1938

Fokker F.VIIb-3 CH-192 photographed in Abyssinia (now Ethiopia)

The fast Lockheed Orion gave Swissair a temporary advantage over the competition

Swiss revolution

On 1 April 1932, Zimmermann, in agreement with the *Eidgenössisches Luftamt*, had ordered two Lockheed 9B Orion, then the fastest transport aircraft in the world, with a maximum speed of 360 km/h and a cruising speed of 270km/h. The rationale behind the acquisition of the Orion was Zimmermann's belief that speed would be his trump card against road and rail travel. The acquisition caused some raised eyebrows in the international community, which had been getting used to demands for three-engined aircraft for improved safety, and here was a revolutionary single-engined type destined for a route over the Alps. In the event, concerns about safety and suitability proved unfounded. Both aircraft, CH-167 and CH-168, reregistered HB-LAH and HB-LAJ when Switzerland changed its civil registration system on 1 October 1934, were shipped to Zurich, where they arrived at Dübendorf on 7 April 1932.

After simultaneous assembly, a series of trial flights were begun on 22 April with Walter Mittelholzer, Franz Zimmer-

mann and Ernst Nyffenegger at the controls. Following their introduction to the press on 28 April, the Orions were introduced on the Basle-Zurich-Munich-Vienna express route on 1 May, Swissair becoming the first and only airline in Europe to operate this new American aircraft. The introduction of the Orion reduced the journey to Vienna from almost four hours 55 minutes to two hours and 40 minutes. The *Rote Hund* (Red Hound), as it was nicknamed due to its distinctive all-red livery, was also put onto the Zurich-Paris and the Zurich-Stuttgart-Leipzig/Halle-Berlin routes the following year. Although passengers had to pay a CHF 10 surcharge for flying in the Orion, the aircraft proved so popular that most of its flights were fully booked. In its first year, its average load factor was 74.9 per cent. The Orions proved to be extremely reliable, with the only incident occurring on a flight from Zurich to Geneva, when mud from Dübendorf was thought to have clogged up the retractable undercarriage, which could not be lowered. Fortunately, the belly landing was made without injuries to

Lockheed Orion HB-LAH, formerly CH-167, on the ground at Dübendorf

Curtiss AT-32 C Condor in flight over Lanzenhäusern

Both Lockheed Orions flying over the Glatt between Schwarzenbach and Dübendorf

the passengers. One aircraft was also extensively used on *Alpenflüge*, joyrides over the Alps, and for demonstration purposes outside Switzerland. One such flight was a non-stop journey to Tunis on 20 May, to show the advantages of a fast airliner in the speedy delivery of mail from Europe to Africa. The flight was made by Walter Mittelholzer and mechanic Heinrich Hufschmied in CH-168. Another long-distance flight in the same aircraft and with the same crew was made on 28 April 1934 to Istanbul, a distance of 4,500km covered in five stages.

The Orion 9B was the last wooden monoplane produced by the Lockheed Aircraft Corporation at Burbank and the first commercial aircraft to feature a retractable undercarriage. The Swissair 9B was powered by a single 429 kW (575 hp) Wright R-1820 Cyclone radial engine and had a range of 900 km at a cruising speed of 270 km/h. Accommodation was provided for four passengers, rather than the normal six, to leave room for baggage and mail. Their end in Swissair service came in rather controversial fashion. In a complex deal, Swissair sold the two Orions, plus the Douglas DC-2-115D, HB-ISA, and the Clark GA-43, HB-LAM, to a dubious company headed by a Swiss-Russian antique and art dealer, Vladimir Rosenbaum, who sold them on to a fake French company created to buy aircraft for the Spanish Republican Air Force for use in the bloody Spanish Civil War. The Orions were used on liaison and transport duties but did not survive the civil war.

While the Orion provided the much-desired speed, it was lacking in capacity and Swissair opted for two more unusual American aircraft types, neither of which proved more than a limited success

with Swissair. Having discarded a plan to obtain a Douglas DC-1, on 11 April 1934, it purchased a single Curtiss AT-32 C Condor II, CH-170, a twin-engine two-bay biplane of mixed construction with a retractable landing gear. Built specifically for Swissair, the AT-32 C had the advantage of accommodating 15 passengers and enabled the introduction of a stewardess. It was powered by two 503 kW (675 hp) Wright Cyclone SR-1820-F3 air-cooled supercharged engines and had a cruising speed of 235 km/h and a range of 800 km. It entered service with Swissair on 1 May on the prestigious Zurich-Stuttgart-Leipzig/Halle-Berlin service,

Balz Zimmermann, Pilot Franz Zimmermann, Dr Bierbaum, Walter Mittelholzer and Councillor Baumann on the occasion of the Orion's Zurich-Vienna express line

Cockpit of the Curtiss AT-32 C Condor CH-170

carrying Nellie Hedwig Diener, Europe's first stewardess. This gave the airline considerable, if short-lived, kudos. On 27 July that same year, the Curtiss tragically crashed on the flight from Berlin to Zurich into a forest between Wurmlingen and Tuttlingen on approach to Stuttgart/ Echterdingen and caught fire. All persons on board, including the pilot Armin Mühlematter, radio operator Hans Daschinger, stewardess Nelly Diener, and nine passengers lost their lives. It was Nelly Diener's 80th flight

and earned her the sobriquet *Engel der Lüfte* (angel of the air). It was the first fatal commercial accident in the history of Swiss aviation. The Condor was flying in a thunderstorm at about 3,000 m attitude when the right-wing structure failed and separated from the aircraft. It was believed that the accident was caused by defective construction and metal fatigue. It had been allocated the reregistration HB-LAP, but the crash prevented it being taken up.

Swissair also bought a Clark GA-43 from General

Clark GA-43 and Curtiss AT-32 C Condor

Clark GA-43 CH-169 at Vienna-Aspern

The Clark GA-43 HB-ITU crashed on the Rigi in April 1936

Aviation, registered CH-169 and later HB-LAM, which was shipped to Cherbourg, assembled and flown to Dübendorf on 16 March 1934. It was used principally on the services to Frankfurt and Vienna. It was the first all-metal aircraft in the Swissair fleet, also had a retractable undercarriage, and another attraction was the onboard radio communication installation. Another plus were the five separate metal fire-proof compartments in the wings and fuselage for mail, freight and baggage. Powered by a single 522 kW (700 hp) Wright Cyclone R-1820 engine, which generated a speed of 240 km/h, the GA-43 had accommodation for 10 passengers. A second aircraft, HB-ITU, was acquired on 19 March 1935, but this crashed on 30 April 1936 into the 1,798 m high Rigi mountain on a Frankfurt-Basle cargo flight, with the loss of both occupants, the pilot Ernst Gerber and radio navigator Arthur Müller. It was said that the crew lost orientation due to low visibility while flying in fog at night.

Twin-engined safety

A major fleet modernisation was implemented with the acquisition of six Douglas DC-2, one of the most modern twin-engined airliners with seating for 14 passengers

Swissair's first stewardess Nelly Diener in the cabin of the Clark GA-43 CH-169

in a noise insulated cabin and provision for a stewardess and facilities for preparing food and refreshments. All six Swissair aircraft were built in the Netherlands by Fokker, who had negotiated the sales and manufacturing rights for Europe for USD 100,000. Only one, HB-ISA, was acquired second-hand, having previously been operated for Austrian Chancellor, Engelbert Dollfuss, as A-500. The first aircraft, HB-ITI, was delivered on 4 December 1934,

Douglas DC-2 HB-ITA over Sundgau in the Department Haut-Rhin

and the new type entered service on a new route from Zurich to London/Croydon, via Basle, on 1 April 1935, becoming Swissair's first over-water service. The 725-km leg from Basle was among the longest regular non-stop services in Europe. The DC-2 enabled Swissair to graduate to an all-year-round operation from the winter of 1935/36. The Zurich-Basle-London service developed into the most prestigious route and represented the financial backbone of the entire operation. In February 1938, HB-ISI made the first direct flight from London to St Moritz/Samedan, the highest airport in Europe.

The DC-2 was the successor to the DC-1, of which only one was produced. Powered by two 652 kW (875 hp) Wright R-1820-F2 Cyclone radial piston engines, it had a maximum speed of 340 km/h and a range of 1,600 km. The Swissair aircraft were equipped with five radio aerials, two of which were used for the Lorenz Beam blind-landing radio navigation system, a forerunner of today's Instrument Landing System (ILS), which had been installed at Dübendorf; only the second such system after Berlin/Tempelhof. Swissair had placed great value on the instruction of its pilots in blind-landing, especially during poor weather conditions, and the DC-2 provided additional safety. Three aircraft were lost in accidents, although none through inclement weather. There were no casualties, when HB-ITI failed to get airborne at Zurich/Dübendorf on a flight to London on 28 February 1936, crossed a road and came to rest in a field, suffering substantial damage. Three crew, including the captain, Egon Frei, and two passengers, were not so lucky when HB-ITA struck a hill near Senlis on approach in low visibility to Paris/Le Bourget on 7 January 1939. Eight passengers escaped unhurt. The third aircraft,

HB-ISI, was lost during the war. One aircraft, HB-ITE, remained in the Swissair fleet until sold to South Africa as ZS-DFW on 18 March 1952.

A rather odd choice was the order for a single 10-seat Junkers Ju 86 B-0, powered by two 447 kW (600 hp) Jumo 205C heavy-oil engines, which did not prove a success with the airline. The aircraft, HB-IXI, was delivered on 1 April 1936 and entered service on 7 May on the Zurich-Frankfurt night mail service. It crash-landed already on 12 August that year near Wixhausen, Germany. Although repaired by Junkers, the German manufacturer sent a different aircraft

THe Douglas DC-2 had 14 exclusively window seats

Swissair's first Douglas DC-2 HB-ITI flying over Eschenbach, Lake Zurich and Schmerikon

Junkers JU 86 HB-IXA and Douglas DC-2 at Dübendorf

as a replacement, a Ju 86 B-1, which was delivered on 16 March 1937 and registered HB-IXE. It was reregistered HB-IXA on 8 February 1939, after being refitted with the more reliable BMW 132 petrol engine and redesignated Ju 86 Z11. It operated for only a short while, being damaged beyond repair in a crash-landing after an engine fire near Constance on the Vienna-Zurich service on 20 July 1939. The longest-serving captain and well-known aviation author, Walter Ackermann, mechanic Anton Mannhart, and four passengers lost their lives.

On 30 March 1937, Swissair acquired the operations of the Ostschweizerische Aero-Gesellschaft St Gallen, generally

Hopfner HV 6/28 CH-186 of Aero-St Gallen

Ex-Balair Fokker-Grulich F.III CH-155 of Aero St Gallen operated between 1927 and 1929

Junkers Ju 86 HB-IXA had a short life with Swissair being damaged beyond repair in a crash-landing on the Veinna-Zurich service

Aero St Gallen DH.89 Dragon Six CH-287

de Havilland DH.89 Dragon Six HB-ARA

known as Aero St Gallen, which had been founded at St Gallen/Breitfeld on 25 July 1927 and started operations on 1 August with the Fokker-Grulich F.III CH-155, bought from Balair. The new company initially limited its activities to air-taxi services and sightseeing flights over St Gallen, Lake Constance and the Säntis, a legendary 2.502 m high mountain with a 360° panoramic view over six countries, but soon added a feeder service between St Gallen and Zurich/Dübendorf and Basle, to provide a timely connection with international flights by Ad Astra and Balair. The F.III was written off in an accident on 22 March 1929 and was replaced on 24 April 1929 by a Hopfner HV 6/28, CH-186, a high-wing strut-braced monoplane with a fully enclosed cabin for six passengers, powered by a single 180 kW (240 hp) Walter Castor engine. This was broken up on 23 April 1931 and replaced five days later by the Klemm I.26 St V CH-284, later reregistered HB-ARE, a two-seat low-wing

monoplane, powered by a single Argus As 8 engine, which remained in service until destroyed in an accident on 16 September 1936.

In 1931, the company had moved its operations to Altenrhein, close to Lake Constance. From 1933, it operated a scheduled St Gallen-Zurich-Bern route, jointly with Alpar, Fluggenossenschaft Bern. This service was flown between 1 May and 31 October each year. Aero St Gallen also briefly added the Stinson Voyager, HB-ARH, to its fleet, and on 19 July 1934, started operating the de Havilland D.H.89 Dragon Six, CH-287, which was quickly given the new HB-ARA registration. This was the prototype that had only flown for the first time on 17 April and led to the highly successful D.H.89A Dragon Rapide series of regional airliners. Powered by two 150 kW (200 hp) de Havilland Gipsy Six engines, it had a top speed of 250 km/h and provided accommodation for a pilot and

Two variations of markings on the Douglas DC-3s HB-IRA and HB-IRI

Freight and baggage being loaded onto Douglas DC-3 HB-IRA

Wartime neutrality livery on DC-3 HB-IRI, marked by red and white bands on the forward and rear fuselage, and on each wing

eight passengers. The D.H.89 was the only aircraft taken over from Aero St Gallen by Swissair, where it received yet another new registration, HB-APA, also becoming the first British aircraft to enter service with the airline on 1 May 1937 on the route Zurich-St Gallen/ Altenrhein-Munich.

Quantum leap

A major step-up in Swissair's capacity was implemented with an order for two Douglas DC-3 aircraft from Fokker, HB-IRA and HB-IRI, which went into service on 10 and 22 June 1937 respectively, introducing a non-stop Zurich-London service, one of the longest routes at the time. The upgrade in capacity was necessary, as the DC-2 was no longer adequate and Swissair had to put in many extra flights to meet demand. Fitted with a right-hand door, the new flagship, developed from the DC-2 with a wider and longer fuselage, greater wingspan, stronger landing gear and more power, although still unpressurised, provided accommodation for up to 28 passengers. It was powered by two 746 kW (1,000 hp) Wright R-1820 Cyclone engines, providing a maximum speed 370 km/h and a range of 2,500 km, and quickly established an enviable reputation with Swissair and other operators. Both were later refitted with the more powerful 820 kW (1,100 lb) G-102A Cyclone engines. Sadly, that same year, Swissair said goodbye to its two founding members, both Swiss aviation pioneers. On 9 May, Walter Mittelholzer died in a climbing accident in Austria, and Balz Zimmermann passed away through illness on 13 October. Henri Pillichody, then director and chief pilot of Berne-based Alpar, was named the new technical director from 1 February 1938, and Eugen Groh was nominated as commercial director.

Swissair obtained two more aircraft, HB-IRE and HB-IRO and a fifth, HB-IRU, in 1938/39, with the more powerful G-102 Cyclone engines. HB-IRU arrived at Dübendorf in Switzerland on 10 August 1939, just three weeks before the outbreak of World War Two. Although Swissair had no need for a fifth DC-3, it was forced into the acquisition by the *Eidgenössische Luftamt,* which had envisaged a requirement for an aircraft to be available to transport important government

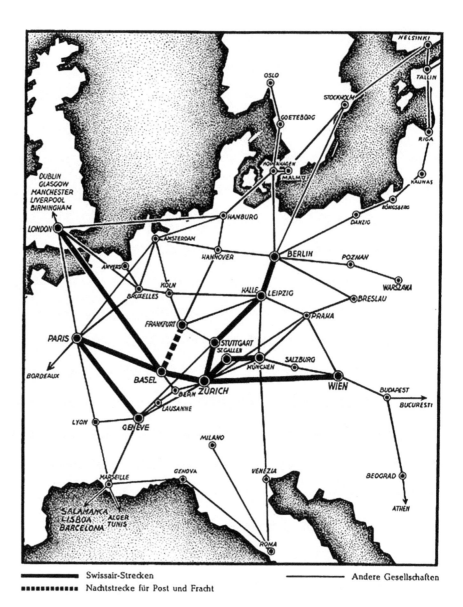

Route map in Central Europe. Swissair routes in thick black lines, including a night service for mail and freight shown by a broken line

officials during a war emergency. However, Swissair received a sweetener in the form of the promise of a CHF 350,000 subsidy. Apart from test flights on 13 and 14 October 1939, undertaken by Walter Borner and Otto Heitmanek, who were on leave from the Swiss Army, the aircraft languished unused in the Dübendorf hangar. Swissair never obtained a Certificate of Airworthiness for this DC-3, and without it, the subsidy did not materialise. The only option for Swissair was to dispose of the aircraft.

At the time, Swedish airline AB Aerotransport, which had been operating from Stockholm to Zurich via Copenhagen and Berlin with Junkers Ju 52/3ms since 1 June, was on the lookout for additional aircraft to service the proposed courier run between neutral Sweden and Scotland. It is not known how the DC-3 came into the picture, but in April 1940, Carl Florman and his Swissair counterpart, Eugen

Douglas DC-3 HB-IRO in neutrality livery at Locarno/Magadino

Wartime Douglas DC-3 and Douglas DC-2 HB-ITO in the background

Groh, forged a deal under which HB-IRU would join the ABA fleet for CHF 750,000. Both were happy with this outcome, especially Swissair, which made a handsome profit on the transaction. However, Swissair's unilateral move without reference to the *Luftamt*, caused considerable consternation and, on 4 May 1940, General Henri Guisan, head of the Swiss Army, wrote to the *Bundesrat*, vehemently objecting to the sale and the granting of an export licence, suggesting that the aircraft could be bought with military funds, or be taken over by the State. But the Swedes had one ace up their sleeves. On 22 January, the Swiss government had placed a CHF 3 million order for 500 tonnes of gunpowder from Swedish manufacturer AB Bofors-Nobelkrut for the army's 105 mm artillery system, and this was now made conditional on the delivery of the DC-3 to Sweden. As the munition was required urgently, the General accepted defeat and the export order was granted on 15 May.

Douglas DC-3 HB-IRU, AB Aerotransport title and the name *Gripen*

But obtaining the rights to fly across Germany to deliver the DC-3 to Sweden, was yet another hurdle to overcome. Carl Florman had already had dinner with Reichsmarshall Hermann Göring in Berlin on 19 April and, after tough negotiations, came away not only with a re-affirmation of the continuance of ABA's scheduled passenger services to Germany, but also with permission to ferry the Swissair aircraft across German airspace to Sweden. On 20 May, with the hastily applied Swedish registration SE-BAG, Ernst Algot Lindberg took the DC-3 into the air and headed for Stockholm/Bromma, making a refuelling stop at Berlin/Tempelhof on the way. On 22 October 1943, it was shot down by a Luftwaffe Junkers Ju 88 C-6 over the Skagerrak. The remaining four Swissair DC-3s survived the war.

Comte AC-4 Gentleman HB-IKO at Dübendorf in wartime

The de Havilland DH.89 was one of three aircraft left at Dübendorf during the war while all the others were evacuated to the Tessin

Europe at war

As elsewere in Europe, air transport ceased completely as war became inevitable. On 24 February 1939 the Swiss Federal Council determined that in case of mobilisation of the military, Swiss airspace would be automatically closed. This came into effect on 28 August with the mobilisation of the border force of the Swiss Army. The army command, however, allowed special flights within the country, and the airports on the border, including St Gallen/Altenrhein, Geneva/Cointrin and the newly-opened airport of Locarno/Magadino, could accept flights from abroad with special permission. On 27 August, with the airspace over Germany and France closed, the services to Amsterdam, which had only been re-activated on 16 April via Basle and Rotterdam in pool with KLM, and those to Paris and London, had to be discontinued and all other services ceased on 29 August. The abrupt cessation of all flying activity hit the airline hard, especially as the summer season had begun with great promise. In spite of great efforts, it was not possible to resume its schedules, even in a reduced form. The Swissair fleet, fully refuelled in case of a need of a quick evacuation, was hidden away in the hangars. With the terminal painted in dark green camouflage and the runway mined, the airport of Zurich/Dübendorf lost its civil character.

In January 1940, after repeated requests by Swissair, the army command gave permission for the reinstatement of scheduled services from Locarno/Magadino, which was situated on the southern side of the Alps, initially only to Barcelona, via Milan, and to Rome. However, the difficult diplomatic negotiations with the Italian and Spanish authorities delayed the first service to Rome until 18 March 1940, and to Barcelona until 1 April. A shuttle service to the airport had to be established from Bellinzona. Barcelona was served with the DC-3 and Rome with the DC-2, both of which had to be repainted with red-white neutrality markings on the forward and rear fuselages. The primitiv facilities at Locarno had to be quickly improved to handle these large aircraft. Passengers on these flights were mainly diplomats and Jewish emigrants, and it is known that much gold was also transported. A single ticket to Rome cost CHF 25 (then USD 26), and CHF 200 (USD 207) to Barcelona.

With the German invasion of Western Europe on 10 May 1940, Switzerland, fearing a similar attack by the *Wehrmacht*, initiated its second mobilisation the following day. Its caution was justified as it is known that Hitler was planning an invasion under the codename of *Tannenbaum*. The entire Swissair management and operation was evacuated to the Tessin with the assistance of the army between 14 and 20 May. All DC-2 and DC-3 aircraft were transferred to Locarno or Geneva, and only three older types - the Comte AC-4 HB-IKO, Fokker F.VIIa HB-LBO and de Havilland D.H.89 Dragon Six HB-APA - were left

The DH.98 Mosquito made an emergency landing at Berne on 24 August 1942 and was eventually 'loaned' to Swissair on 13 October 1944 and given the registration HB-IMO

behind at Dübendorf. Already on 22 May, some Swissair management functions were returned to Zurich, while the technical operation was accommodated in a manufacturing facility at Bodio. With Italy's entry into the war on the side of Germany on 10 June, the Barcelona and Rome services had to be suspended, Barcelona on 18 June and Rome on 25 June. After a heightened tension through repeated violations of Swiss airspace by Nazi Germany, when two military aircraft were shot down by the Luftwaffe on 4 and 6 June with the loss of three Swiss pilots, the situation eased somewhat. Swissair was ordered to return to Dübendorf, a move that was completed between 7 and 16 August 1940, thus ending three months of evacuation.

Following lengthy and often difficult discussions with the German authorities, Swissair was able to open a service between St Gallen/Altenrhein and Munich on 30 September 1940, and between 2 and 14 January 1941, a few fights were once again operated from Locarno to Rome. On 14 November 1941, the German authorities rescinded their agreement for the Munich route, but in recompense, Swissair was offered a licence on the Zurich-Stuttgart-Berlin route. This was started on 19 November and operated until

29 January 1943, when Germany insisted that the service was to terminate at Stuttgart, which was maintained from 30 January 1943 until 17 August 1944. In addition, Swissair was able to obtain authorisation for nine special flights between Stuttgart and Berlin and vice versa for the transport of important delegations. These ceased in April 1944.

On 9 August 1944, Swissair lost Douglas DC-2 HB-ISI on the ground at Stuttgart/Echterdingen in an air attack by USAAF Lockheed P-38 Lightning fighter aircraft, and all flights were discontinued on 17 August. The uncertain outlook for the future during the war ensured that few improvements were intiated at Dübendorf. The most notable were the installation, as early as 1942, of runway lighting to ease landing at night and in inclement weather, and the construction of buildings for Swissair's technical operation and for the training of pilots and radio operators. The fact that the airline, in spite of massively reduced flying activities and few financial resources, embarked on these projects was a clear indication that it was already preparing for life in the post-war years. One move towards that aim was an increase in capital to CHF 1 million.

The war brought an unusual aircraft into the Swissair fleet for a short time. On 24 August 1942, the British Lieutenant Wooll of No.1 PRU of the Royal Air Force was forced to shut down one of the engines on his de Havilland DH.98 Mosquito, serial DK 310, a multitole combat aircraft, on a flight over Venice due to overheating. Realising that he could not make it back to Britain, he landed his aircraft at Berne/Belpmoos. Although Switzerland was neutral in the war, Britain was determined that the Mosquito should not fall into the hands of the Luftwaffe, but the Swiss military took control and prevented its destruction. On 1 August 1943, Switzerland and Britain agreed that the aircraft would be allowed to fly under the Swiss registration of E-42 and was used for test flights by the Swiss *Fliegertruppe* until "loaned" to Swissair in October 1944. Swissair employed the Mosquito on night airmail flights from January 1945 and also on pilot training with the registration HB-IMO. It was returned to the military at the end of the war.

On 20 September 1944, DC-2 HB-ITE, flown by Otto Heitmanek with radio operator Jost Guyer, had made a special flight over the route Zurich-Berne-Geneva-Lausanne, to commemorate the 25th Anniversary of the Swiss Post Office. The return flight made stops at the same destinations. Records indicate that Swissair made a net profit of CHF 241,842 from this flight. Other, much-needed income was generated for a time by the airline's technical operation, through third-party contracts from the Swiss Army, Dornier (manufacture of aircraft parts) and Deutsche Lufthansa. The work for Lufthansa involved eleven aircraft, which included four DC-2 and three DC-3 captured from KLM Royal Dutch Airlines, and four DC-3 from Czechoslovakia's ČSA. The third-party work generated a much-needed profit of CHF 135,226 in 1942, and a gross income of CHF 170,000 in 1943. However, the Federal Council prohibited Swissair from continuing this activity in December 1943. The Swissair third-party work, especially that for Dorniet and Lufthansa, had brought into sharp focus the questionable neutrality of the country.

Children in the clouds

The childhood bacterial infection of whooping cough, also known as pertussis, was prevalent throughout the world. By the time of the outbreak of the Second World War, there was no effective vaccine available and antibiotics had yet to be developed. The medical profession experimented with various treatments, one of which suggested a period at high altitude would relieve and even cure the symptoms. With Swissair's light unpressurised aircraft, the de Havilland DH.89, Fokker F.VIIa and Comte AC-4 having been relegated to Alpine sightseeing flights and aerial photography, the airline introduced the so-called Keuchhustenflüge (whooping cough flights) in 1940 from Zurich/ Dübendorf. With open windows, children, generally up to 12-years of age, accompanied by a parent or nurse, were taken up to 3,000m altitude, where the aircraft circled, before landing after about one hour in the air. Flights only took place in good weather. For a flight with eight persons, a fare of CHF 40 per person was charged, for six persons it was CHF 50, with CHF 45 in a two-seat aircraft. According to medical statistics, in 80 per cent of cases a noticeable improvement or cure of whooping cough after the altitude flight could be detected. Swissair discontinued these flights in 1943.

Swissair Operational Statistics (Scheduled Services) 1931-1945

Figures for 1939 are 1 January-31 August; for 1945 from 30 July-31-December

YEAR	PASSENGERS	BAGGAGE Kg	FREIGHT Kg	MAIL Kg	Km FLOWN
1931	10,282	102,527	170,871	84,065	724,476
1932	11,833	123,872	149,671	61,016	670,436
1933	13,003	134,192	131,850	97,824	761,100
1934	17,764	194,165	94,398	60,213	836,391
1935	24,642	295,539	134,651	90,912	1,045,072
1936	21,485	311,223	92,746	80,678	1,055,635
1937	31,344	442,314	126,343	155,444	1,415,098
1938	35,249	504,395	136,309	341,348	1,483,794
1939	28,331	391,194	102,087	306,445	1,189,913
1940	1,613	33,642	14,201	7,460	248,880
1941	3,922	70,750	44,253	36,296	202,966
1942	16,232	228,440	123,840	148,119	491,522
1943	4,736	80,077	63,322	72,326	150,188
1944	2,181	49,106	29,773	61,451	75,376
1945	10,144	179,336	83,538	78,411	376,140

A phalanx of military aircraft at Dübendorf during World War Two

Starting again

Swissair survived the war relatively unscathed, with only minimal losses sustained in a few of the war years. At the end of the war on 8 May 1945, the Swissair fleet comprised nine aircraft, including two Douglas DC-2, HB-ITE and HB-ITO; four DC-3, HB-IRA, HB-IRE, HB-IRI, and HB-IRO; the Comte AC-4 Gentleman, HB-IKO; de Havilland DH.89 Dragon Six, HB-APA; and the Fokker VIIa, HB-LBO. Scheduled passenger services to the European capitals were quickly re-established, starting with Paris from Zurich and Geneva on 30 July 1945 with six flights a week in pool with Air France; Amsterdam on 19 September, three times a week; and London on 29 September, until 4 November flown three times a week. From the following day, the frequency was increased to four weekly flights, with Geneva added to the schedule with two flights a week. Additional income was generated by a number of special flights, which included three from Geneva to Lisbon, eight from Geneva to Barcelona, one from Geneva to Tunis, 13 from Zurich to London, and 11 from Zurich to Malmö, with a refuelling stop at Amsterdam.

New aircraft were required to enable Swissair to add further destinations to its once again growing network. While new-generation aircraft were then still in the prototype stage, the airline opted for an interim solution trough the acquisition of nine Douglas DC-3/C-47 aircraft. However, Swissair was only available to obtain two brand-new DC-3D from Douglas, HB-IRB and HB-IRC, which went into service on 15 February and 29 May 1946

respectively, it also bought seven C-47 models in good condition from surplus US Army Air Force (USAAF) stock. Four of these underwent a thorough conversion to passenger configuration at Prestwick in Scotland, two were turned into freighters, and one was acquired for spare parts. The first three C-47B variants also entered service in 1946, with the other three following a year later.

The network was boosted on 8 January 1946 with new services to Prague, Brussels and Warsaw, followed on 13 April with a Zurich-Amsterdam-Malmö route, although the latter was rerouted Zurich-Copenhagen-Stockholm from 12 October. Geneva was also connected to Lisbon via Barcelona from April 1946, and with Brussels from 1 May. A new Basle-Amsterdam night mail and freight service was flown between 1 August and 5 October. A new Zurich-Basle-London freight service was added in 1947. New routes in 1948 included Bern-London from 14 June to 18 September, and Zurich-Manchester from 11 December. Some Geneva-Lydda-Cairo and Zurich-Cairo services were extended to Basra, Iraq, to meet special requirements. Swissair also continued its extensive series of intercontinental trial flights, which, in 1948, included 17 more flights to New York from Geneva and four from Zurich, and 20 additional flights from Geneva to Johannesburg. In the same year, the Fokker VIIa, HB-LBO, was taken out of service because of a lack of spare parts.

On 14 June 1948, particular aircraft started flying from the new Zurich airport of Kloten, and on 17 November, Dübendorf was closed to all scheduled flights.

A new Douglas DC-3D HB-IRB entered service in 1946

The DH.89A Dragon Rapide was taken over from Alpar in 1947. It was previously registered as HB-AME

The Zurich Airports

The airport at Dübendorf was established as a civil airfield in 1910 and was leased and expanded by the military, before being taken over by the government in 1918. Although it served as the starting point for the trial flights for mail in 1919 and a scheduled passenger service was inaugurated by Ad Astra in 1922, it remained essentially a military airport. At first, commercial flights were undertaken from Zürichhorn with seaplanes and from Schwamendingen-Mattenhof with landplanes. As civil air transport began to establish a firm foothold at Dübendorf, a civil infrastructure was created, with the building of temporary hangars and a wooden terminal. The military, however, found the civil residents a nuisance until the military department and the government agreed a three-year leasing contract that ensured the co-existence of civil and military transport. However, relations remained fractious throughout. As a direct result of the Great Depression, an ambitious plan for a large, all-encompassing terminal building, new hangars and other infrastructure, was watered down, and, on 16 July 1932, the new civil area was opened to traffic and included a terminal, a hangar for two aircraft, a maintenance workshop and a hangar for general aviation. Two-thirds of the area was now taken up by the military, and one-third by civil activities, with

both under separate management. The grass runway was used by both. With traffic more than doubling over the following seven years, some expansion was undertaken, which included a new 500 m concrete runway. By the outbreak of the Second World War, Dübendorf was served by eight airlines and had reached saturation. The runway at Dübendorf was then extended to 1,100 m with steel plates provided by the US Army. Following a decision by the Federal Council of 22 June 1945, determined efforts were made to expand and improve the airports for Zurich, Geneva and build new regional airports. After grandiose plans for a Swiss central airport had been dismissed in favour of building a new airport for Zurich at Kloten to serve as Switzerland's main airport, a project was unveiled on 31 December 1943, which envisaged four concrete runways of 2,000 m, 1,800 m, 1,700 m and 1,450 m in length and all 45 m wide. This was replaced on 29 April 1944 with another, more modest, proposal with reduced runway lengths and smaller total area, which cut the budgeted construction cost from CHF 87 million to 65 million. This too was rejected and replaced on 31 July 1944 with a third project that further reduced the cost to CHF 54.4 million. This was again developed to propose yet more differing runway lengths and widths and was formally adopted on 5 May 1946. After more delays and changes

Dübendorf Airport in 1947

Aerial view and airside of Zurich/Kloten

to the plans, the first 1,900 m west runway at Kloten was officially opened on 14 June 1948 and was first used by a Swissair DC-4 on the service to London. On 17 November, the 2,600 m long runway equipped for instrument landing was put into operation, a new maintenance centre was opened, and all flights were transferred from Dübendorf to Zurich/Kloten. A new terminal building was completed on 9 April 1953. A major expansion plan introduced in 1957 to take account of the impending introduction of jet aircraft,

primarily involved the extensions of the West and ILS runways, which were put into operation on 1 January and 15 March 1961 respectively, the expansion of the terminal complex, and the construction of two finger piers. Several more stages of construction followed over the next 50 years, and the airport today has three airside Terminals A, B and E, which are linked to the central Airside Centre, and three runways of 3,700 m, 3,300 m and 2,500 m in length.

Convair 240 named *Glarus* in flight over the Alps

Convair 240 HB-IRT was one of four sold to Mohawk Airlines in the United States after seven years of service with Swissair

The necessary modernisation of the fleet had been continued in July 1947 with an order for four pressurised Convair 240 twin-piston aircraft, although these were not delivered to Zurich until February/March 1949. Designed initially as a DC-3 replacement, the attractive low-wing monoplane was powered by two 1,800 kW (2.400 hp) Pratt & Whitney R-2800-CA3 Double Wasp air-cooled radial piston engines with exhaust thrust augmentation, capable of a maximum speed of 505 km/h, and a range of 1,900 km. The pressurised cabin provided accommodation for 40 passengers, which was a considerable improvement over the DC-3 on the busier European routes. Other features were a tricycle landing gear, a ventral airstair for passenger boarding, and a number of other door options including forward starboard main door with integral airstair, and a starboard rear cargo door. Their entry into service in April 1949 enabled the opening of several new direct flights in

Europe, substantially increasing operations. These were further boosted by 63 flights between Geneva and New York from 29 April, three flights extending from Cairo to Bombay (now Mumbai), and two further special flights to Johannesburg, although permission for the latter was withdrawn by the South African Government in March. Other important events were the opening of the expansion of Geneva/Cointrin on 22 May and the construction of an engine test facility at Zurich/Kloten.

State support

The first years after the war, Swissair limited its operations to European destinations, and, in contrast to the *Luftamt*, was averse to enter into the intercontinental market. In a government called conference on 7 March 1946, to which Swissair and Alpar, the Berne-based airline, were invited, the development of Switzerland's air transport was discussed, but the government was adamant that this should not be limited to Europe but should also secure the country's place in intercontinental traffic. It suggested that the great efforts required, such as the acquisition of newer and larger aircraft and the recruitment of additional personnel, would best be achieved through a merger between Swissair and Alpar, to establish a single flagship airline, thus eliminating the competition between the two. Towards this aim, Alpar increased its capital by CHF 1.2 million, and Swissair planned an increase of CHF 19 million, which it said was necessary to keep pace with the economic development and growing demand, as well as the technical advances and

increasing competition in the international market. It also placed an order for four-engined 44-seat Douglas DC-4-1009, the newest airliner to emerge from the United States.

A general assembly on 12 February confirmed the increase of the capital from CHF 1 million to CHF 20 million. In the end, the government opted for the development of Swissair as the national airline. Alpar lost out in its battle with the larger Swissair and was stopped from providing scheduled passenger flights from 18 August 1947 and was liqidated later that year. Some personnel and a single Douglas DC-3, HB-ATI, and two de Havilland D.H.89A Dragon Rapide biplanes, HB-AME and HB-APU, were taken over by

Douglas DC-4-1009 HB-ILA on home turf and over New York

DC-4 HB-ILO at Dakar on first South America flight in October 1947

Swissair at a cost of CHF 664,000. HB-ATI and HB-AME were reregisterd HB-IRX and HB-APE respectively in Swissair service. Another C-47, HB-ASA, was taken over and used for spares.

Various private and state entities participated in Swissair's capital increase, including the City and Canton of Geneva, with, respectively, 1,000 and 2,000 shares of CFH 500 each, which wanted to ensure the interest of Geneva and its airport, then the only airport, which could be served with long-range aircraft. Other state-owned participants were the Swiss Railways (*Schweizerische Bundesbahnen*-SBB), the Post, Telephone and Telegraph agency (*Post-, Telefon- und Telegrafenbetriebe*-PTT), and more Cantons, bringing the state holding to 30.6 per cent.

Swissair's first DC-4, HB-ILA landed at Geneva on its delivery flight on 24 November 1946. In December, it made the airline's first long-distance flight to Lydda in Palestine and Cairo, Egypt. There followed a number of intercontinental trial flights, designed to collect information on the necessary commercial and technical requirements, while also assessing the need for appropriate training of flight crew. The first flight was a Geneva-New York service via Shannon, Ireland and Stephenville, Newfoundland, on 1 May 1947 with HB-ILA, although the flight ended up in Washington DC due to fog at New York/La Guardia. During the year, another six flights were completed to New York, one flight was made to Rio de Janeiro and Buenos Aires on 10 October and three flights to Johannesburg, starting on 3 August. In addition, special permission was granted for regular flights over the Geneva-Athens-Lydda-Cairo, Geneva-Athens-Istanbul/Ankara , Geneva-Barcelona and Zurich-Warsaw routes. Tegular scheduled DC-4 services from Geneva to New York were inaugurated on 29 April 1949. It is interesting to note that Swissair did consider buying the Lockheed Constellation, and even allotted a registration HB-IBI for it on 27 August 1949, but this was never taken up.

The DC-4 did not meet expectation and proved uncompetitive, and Swissair made the introduction of regular scheduled intercontinental flights dependent on receiving financial support from the State. While it dropped this demand at the general assembly on 23 September 1949, the airline was severely impacted by the British Sterling Crisis that same year and the devaluation in other countries served. As European air fares were based on the Pound Sterling, its devaluation resulted in a very considerable decline in traffic revenue. With bankruptcy a worrying possibility, Swissair petitioned the Federal Government on 30 March 1950 for support to stave off its possible demise. It also pointed out that it was financially unable to acquire new long-haul aircraft and asked that it would need initially at least two aircraft. In July 1950, the government agreed to buy two pressurised Douglas DC-6B aircraft, which it put at the disposal of Swissair. But Swissair needed more help. On 23 August, the *Bundesrat* (Federal Council) proposed to reduce the airline's amortisation risk and for the government to buy the four DC-4 and Convair 240 aircraft, with Swissair charged to make a financial contribution depending on operational results. This was, however, considered too complicated and was rejected. Instead, a reduction in capital was negotiated, which was to be used to cover the 1949 loss of CHF 3,167,659 and to provide a reserve to cover future depreciation of its aircraft fleet. On 28 September, the acquisition of the two DC-6B was confirmed, and the government also provided up to CHF 500,000 a year for the training of flight crew. The capital was reduced from CHF 20 million to CHF 14 million in an agreement of 10 November.

Another plan to guarantee future support was the creation of a joint Amortisation Fund between Swissair and the government. Swissair's deposit was to be based on the excess of the operating account and was based on the honest depreciation requirement for a seven-year depreciation period. The Federal Government would

Swissair' first Douglas DC-6B was named *Zürich*

The DC-6A Freighter HB-IBB *Uri* entered service in October 1953

make a yearly contribution of CHF 1.5 million, up to a maximum of CHF 15 million. These supporting measures were made retroactive from 1 January 1950 for a period of 10 years, although Swissair had the right to an early optout from the leasing contract for the DC-6B aircraft, and the Amortisation Fund. Both these contracts were signed on 1 May 1951.

New milestone

The acquisition of the two DC-6B, HB-IBA *Zürich* and HB-IBE *Genève*, marked a milestone in the history of Swissair, and the type was put into service on the New York

route on 18 August 1951. Both were bought by Swissair on 31 December 1955. In the night of 30/31 January 1952, HB-IBA had made a fast crossing of the North Atlantic, flying the New York-Geneva route in 10 hours and 24 minutes, making the actual crossing from Gander to Shannon in 4 hours and 36 minutes, both times creating unofficial records for commercial aircraft. Developed from the DC-4, it was the US manufacturer's first pressurised transport and provided accommodation for 69 passengers in Swissair service. The DC-6B had more powerful 1,865 kW (2,500 hp) Pratt & Whitney T-2800-CB17 Double Wasp radial engines, compared to the basic model, and more fuel capacity, increasing the maximum payload range to 4,830 km. The introduction of the DC-6B contributed to a 35 increase in tonne-kilometres. In 1951, Swissair also added a tourist-class to some of its flight on the North Atlantic and Europe. This was risky, as the shortfall in income due to reduced ticket prices, had to be made up through increased traffic.

The arrival of the DC-6B had also been timely, as Swissair had little luck with the DC-4, losing the first aircraft, HB-ILE *Zürich*, already on 13 December 1950. On a flight from Geneva to New York via Gander and Halifax, poor weather forced the crew to divert to Sydney, Nova Scotia. Approaching too low, the aircraft struck three light masts damaging the propellers on Nos. 1 and 2 engines, which failed to arrest the rapid descent, in spite of the application of full power. The DC-4 hit the ground, shearing off the left wing and ground looped before coming to a stop. A small fire broke out, which the crew initially controlled, but re-ignited later and destroyed the entire aircraft. Thankfully, there were no casualties among the 31 persons on board. Nor were there in the accident of HB-ILO *Luzern*, which was damaged beyond repair while attempting an overshoot during an ILS aproach in dense fog to Amsterdam/Schiphol on 14 December 1951. A replacement for HB-ILO, registered HB-ILU, was acquired from Pan American. More DC-6B made up the shortage in the long-haul fleet, with five more acquired between 23 October 1952 and 26 October 1953, and a sixth on 15 June 1958. Swissair also took on a DC-6A Freighter, HB-IBB *Uri* on 2 October that same year. All had left the fleet by 1962.

Although the 1952 summer season was satisfactory, the year was affected by the strike of the US oil industry, which led to drastic cuts in supply, although the Federal Government helped to minimise the reduction in traffic. This was also due to a lack of pilots and led to a 9 per cent reduction in the flying programme, in spite of the employment of foreign crew. Poor weather conditions from September to the end of the year added to the airline's problems. Nevertheless, results from its North Atlantic services were highly satisfactory and justified the acquisition of additional Douglas DC-6B aircraft. It transported 10,091 passengers across the Atlantic, of which 4,259 were in tourist-class, which represented a near doubling over the previous year, and accounted for 31 per cent of revenues. The average load factor was 74.7 per cent. An accident at New York/Idlewild on 10 May 1952, put the DC-6B, HB-IBE *Genève*, out of action for a few months. The parked aircraft suffered much damage to the forward fuselage when it was hit by a Pan American Stratocruiser.

While the growth strategy continued to focus on its long-haul routes, it also opened a promising new route in Europe from Zurich to Rome via Milan. However, its routes to the Middle East, with the exception of that to Istanbul, were below expectation and were impacted by the conflict between the Iranian Government and the Anglo-Iranian Oil Company, which forced a cessation of the route to Abadan. Currency problems in Israel and political difficulties in Egypt did not help either.

The two Douglas DC-2 were no longer suitable for the scheduled network and were sold to Phoenix Airlines of South Africa. Another aircraft no longer required was the single Nord 1000, the French-built single-engine version Messersmitt Bf 108 Taifun, HB-IKI, which had a capacity for four passengers and was used by Swissair for feeder

The single-engine Nord 1000 HB-IKI

Swissair acquired twelve Convair 440 Metropolitan twin-engine aircraft which were configured for 44 passengers with Swissair

flights from 1948. It was sold to the *Eidgenössische Luftamt* on 29 May 1953. The regional fleet was increased with four ex-KLM Convair 240, three of which were delivered in November/December 1953, with the fourth arriving in Switzerland in July the following year. Efforts to obtain transit rights for its North Atlantic services in London and Paris, the so-called fifth freedom rights, to enable an increase in frequencies, were denied by the respective governments. Swissair also followed the development of the helicopter with great interest and, although it considered it too early to acquire such machines, it took a stake in Scheizerische Helikoptergesellschaft.

Highlights of 1954 included, after overcoming extensive

administrative and technical obstacles, the inauguration of a route to South America on 27 May, connecting Zurich and Geneva with Rio de Janeiro and São Paulo, via Dakar and Recife, flying once a week. Swissair was also determined to expand its cargo flights and opened a weeklt service to New York, for which the DC-4, HB-IL., was converted to provide passenger and freight services depending on need. Other long-haul routes to the Middle East were improved with the DC-6B, the airline's biggest and fastest aircraft, which was also put on the London route. The increase in the number of shart-range aircraft also facilitated the expansion of the European network of night flights. Having initially considered acquiring more DC-6B, Swissair

The Convair 440 Metropolitan at Geneva/Cointrin

unsurprisingly opted for the Douglas DC-7C as the next step in its long-range programme. The aircraft's increased range would enable direct flights between Switzerland and the US, reducing the return flight with the DC-6B by some six hours. In a cautious approach, it initially placed an order for two aircraft. The four pre-war Douglas DC-3 were also put up for sale, and the three de Havilland D.H.89 biplanes were no longer economic to operate, even on sightseeing flights, and were also sold.

The loss of Convair 240, HB-IRW, on 19 June 1954, cast a dark shadow over an otherwise successful year. On a flight from Geneva, the Convair ditched in the English Channel near Folkestone after running out of fuel. Although all on board survived the ditching, three people drowned, as they could not swim, and there were no life jackets on board the aircraft. As a result of the accident, Swissair subsequently carried lifesaving equipment on all cross-Channel flights, even though regulations then in force did not require this. Lifesaving equipment only needed to be carried on flights where the time over water exceeded 30 minutes. The investigation into the accident revealed that the aircraft had not been refuelled at Geneva before departing for London.

While the network and fleet remained unchanged in 1955, Swissair made far-reaching plans for the future. With

Douglas DC-7C HB-IBK in flight over the Californian coast

Douglas DC-7C HB-IBL on the ground in Zurich

Swissair leased a British-built Twin Pioneer to evaluate the possibility of introducing feeder flights from high-altitude airports, but decided not to pursue this concept.

the intention of opening a route to the Far East, and to increase frequencies on existing long-haul services, it placed an order for two additional DC-7C, and signed a contract for eight 44-seat Convair 440 Metropolitan aircraft to take over services still performed by the DC-3. Swissair was attracted by the short delivery times of the aircraft, which was the first to be equipped with a weather radar, its additional seating capacity for passengers, increased freight capacity, and the fact that its engines were identical to those of the DC-6B. The total cost of this re-equipment programme for the DC-7C and 440, including spares, was a substantial CHF 100 million, which was partly covered by a decision was made on 26 March 1956 to increase the capital to CHF 42 million, with the State holding remaining at 30.6 per cent. As this tripling of the capital was insufficient to meet its financial obligations, Swissair also took out a loan of CHF 30 million.

The first two DC-7C, HB-IBK *Zürich* and HB-IBL *Genève*, arrived at Zurich on November and December respectively, with the eight Convair 440 also delivered during the year. The three Convair 240 were sold to an American company, but two were leased back for a few months. Weather radars were being installed in the DC-6B fleet. The airline made preparations for the imminent jet age, with an order on 30 January 1956 for two four-engined Douglas DC-8-32 jets, increasing the order to three on 24 September that same year.

Deliveries of new aircraft continued unabated. The third and fourth DC-7C were delivered in 1957, and a fifth ordered, while the Convair 440 fleet was increased by three more. New routes were the first services to the Far East, and the extension of the South America route to Buenos Aires via Montevideo. The first flight to Tokyo with invited guests was made on 1 April, with the first scheduled passenger service opened on 23 April with the DC-6B, routed via Karachi, Bombay, Bangkok and Manila. On the second weekly flight on 5 July, stops were made at Calcutta instead of Bombay, and at Hong Kong in place of Manila. Bahrain was added to the schedule once a week from 1 November 1958, but was itself later replaced by Athens. Also, in April 1957, Swissair opened a weekly service to Dhahran on the Persian Gulf via Beirut and Baghdad. Apart from the direct flights across the North Atlantic, schedules also included Cologne and Lisbon, as Frankfurt could no longer be served.Between January and March 1957, Swissair operated a series of trial flights to the high-altitude airports of Davos, St Moritz, Zermatt and La Chaux-de-Fonds, with a view of evaluating the possibility of adding feeder flights. The aircraft used was a British-built Twin Pioneer, G-AEOE, leased from Scottish Aviation. Although the flight elicited great interest from the public, Swissair decided that a suitable aircraft to meet the economic and technical demands was not yet available, but agreed that it would keep this concept in mind.

Pilot shortage

The Schweizerische Luftverkehrsschule (SLS) (Swiss Air Transport School) was established on 3 October 1958 on the initiative of the Swiss Government with a two-thirds financial participation, to deal with an acute shortage of pilots in the 1950s. SLS was placed under the auspices of Swissair, which had previously undertaken courses for pilot training using a variety of Bücker Bü 31 Jungmann and various Cessna types. After the establishment of SLS with its basis at Zurich/Kloten, several types were leased, including the Piper L 4 Cub and the Bölkow 207, before the new company obtained its own Pilatus P-3, registered HB-HOE. The P-3 was of all-metal construction with a retractable undercarriage and tandem seating, and was powered by a single Lycoming engine. It was designed for primary and advanced training, including night flying, aerobatics and instrument flying. It was sold to the Brazilian Navy in April 1963. The impending introduction of jet aircraft required a

Piper L 4 Cub HB-OUS

SIAT 223 Flamingo HB-EVD

new training aircraft and, after evaluating a number of types, the choice fell on the Piaggio P.149E, an all-metal, low-wing cantilever monoplane with a retractable tricycle landing gear, powered by a single Lycoming engine. The first two, HB-EBV and HB-EBW, arrived at Zurich in May 1961, and to meet demand, a further three P.149E were acquired from Italy, as well as seven P.149D built under licence by Focke-Wulf in Germany.

Pilatus P3 HB-HOE

Focke-Wulf FWP-149D HB-KIU (Hermann Keist)

Douglas DC-3 HB-IRX

Pilatus PC-7 HB-HOO

All were transferred to Hausen am Albis, when SLS relocated to this small village on the southern side of the Albis pass in the Canton of Zurich on 19 July 1963. After removal from scheduled services, Swissair transferred it last three C-47B/DC-3D, HB-IRC, HB-IRN and HB-IRX, on 1 April 1964 to the SLS, where they were used on IFR training, mostly at Zurich and Basle. For basic training, SLS bought the SIAT 223 A1 Flamingo, which was used up to and including PPL (private pilot's licence) between 1968 and 1983, when they were sold to the Farner Werke in Grenchen. The fleet comprised seven standard versions, and three SIAT 223 K1 for aerobatics. The 223 A1 was a conventional low-wing monoplane with a fixed tricycle undercarriage and a single Avco Lycoming engine, used as a two of four-seat trainer, while the 223K1 was used as a single-seat aerobatic aircraft. A contract was signed with the Pilatus Flugzeugwerke on 9 December 1981, whereby the Swiss manufacturer provided a PC-7 for eight weeks of the year for ab initio training. Two different aircraft were used, HB-HOO from 11 August 1992 and HB-HOQ from 07 July 1988. The PC-7 is a highly-successful tandem-seat turbo trainer. Questions were raised in Parliament in October 1995 about Swissair's continued level of pilot training, accusing the airline of knowing that it would not be able to employ these pilots upon completion of their training. Eventually, at the end of 1996, the Swiss Government decided to withdraw its support and cancelled its contract with Swissair. However, operations continued until the last pilots completed their training. SLS was closed down on 30 June 1997. The following year, Swissair set up the Swissair Aviation School AG, taking over some of the SLS aircraft.

Preparing for jets

Based on the flying programme of 1958, it had become clear to Swissair that the three ordered DC-8 long-range jets for delivery in 1960 would be insufficient to compete effectively with other airlines. It was convinced that three different types with ranges for intercontinental traffic, medium routes to the Middle East, and the more important European services, would be the best solution. Swissair also recognised that the financial and technical implications would stretch its resources, and turned to Scandinavian Airlines System (SAS), with which it already had friendly relations. The multi-national SAS had a likewise operating policy, flew similar aircraft, and conducted its business without state subsidies and without state interference in its management. It had also ordered the DC-8. A close co-operation with SAS was, therefore, seen by Swissair as an economic solution for both companies to facilitate the transition to pure jet aircraft. Negotiations were opened at the beginning of 1958 with a view of establishing a strong co-operation, especially with regards to re-equipment policies, aircraft maintenance and training. After thorough analysis of potential benefits to both companies, a 10-year agreement was signed on 6 October 1958, which would result in a reduction of capital investment and improved operational efficiency through a co-ordinated programme of aircraft purchases and joint utilisation of workshops and technical facilities.

As part of the agreement, both airlines placed substantial orders for jet aircraft. It was agreed that SAS and Swissair would introduce the DC-8 for their long-haul routes, the

Caravelle III HB-ICY *Lausanne* was one of four leased from Scandinavian Airlines System (SAS) in 1960

Swissair's first Douglas DC-8-32 HB-IDA *Matterhorn*

The four-engine Douglas DC-8-32 operated all North Atlantic services from 27 September 1960

Convair 880, for medium-haul routes, and the Sud-Aviation SE-210 Caravelle III for high-density European routes and those to Mediterranean destinations. The aircraft would be delivered with identical interiors and standardised equipment, and maintenance and overhaul work would be divided, with SAS taking care of the DC-8 and Caravelle, and Swissair of the Convair 880, of which it ordered five aircraft at a cost of CHF 170 million, including spare parts, on 6 October, together with new infrastructure, and a flight simulator. Two additional aircraft were to be leased to SAS for four years, while SAS ordered four extra Caravelles, which were to be leased to Swissair, also for four years. The training of personnel was also to be jointly organised. Swissair was happy with these arrangements and felt ready to embrace the new jet age. Much-needed extra financial resources were provided through a capital increase to CHF 63 million, and a second loan facility of CHF 30 million, but this was still considered insufficient, and on 9 April 1959, the general assembly agreed to a further capital increase to CHF 105 million.

The introduction of the Sud Aviation SE-210 Caravelle III, HB-ICW named *Solothurn*, on the Zurich-London service on 21 May 1960 marked Swissair's entry into the jet age. Nine days later, on 30 May, the Douglas DC-8-50, HB-IDA *Matterhorn*, followed with its first service to New York. While the Caravelles were scheduled on the services within Europe and to the Middle East, long-haul routes to the Far East and South America were still flown by DC-6B and DC-7C propeller

aircraft. Not so on the North Atlantic, where all flights were scheduled with the DC-8 jet aircraft from 27 September 1960, resulting in a sizeable increase in passenger numbers. Distinctive features of the Caravelle were the rear-mounted engines, which reduced cabin noise, the curved triangular windows, the built-in retractable stairs at the rear, and the deployment of a drogue parachute on earlier models, before the introduction of thrust reversers. The nose section and cockpit layout came directly from the Comet airliner.

Caravelle III HB-ICU *Aargau* and Convair 990-30A Coronado HB-ICB *Luzern*

The Convair 880-22m HB-ICM was one of two operated as an interim measure pending delivery of the bigger and faster 990 Coronado

The first production models, built at Toulouse/Blagnac by Sud-Aviation, formed on 1 March 1957 through the amalgamation of SNCASE and SNCASO, were powered by two 46.7 kN (10,500 lb) Rolls-Royce RA-29 Avon Mk.522 turbojets and provided accommodation for 80 passengers. The three DC-8-32 aircraft delivered in 1960 were powered by four 75.2 kN (16,800 lb) Pratt & Whitney JT4A-9 turbojets and had a range of some 7,400 km, and a cruising speed of 895 km/h. Accommodation was for 132 passengers. In February/March 1961, all three were converted to the DC-8-33 model, with more powerful 78.4 kN (1,500 lb) JT4A-11 engines, a modification to the flap linkage for a more efficient cruise, and stronger landing gear. One aircraft, HB-IDB, was converted to the DC-8-53

and renamed *Genf*. This involved mainly the fitting of the 80.6 kN (18,000 lb) JT3D-3B, an early turbofan engine.

On 30 September 1959, Swissair changed its order for the Convair 880 to the larger and faster four-engined Convair 990A, which it named *Coronado*, adding two more to enable the lease of two to Scandinavian Airlines System (SAS). But with deliveries badly delayed due to under-performance in range and speed and other teething problems, the US manufacturer made available two of the smaller 880-22M versions as an interim measure and at a favourable cost. These were HB-ICL and HB-ICM, which operated successfully on the routes to the Middle East and Far East in the summer of 1961. Both were returned on 19 May 1962, by which time four Coronado had been

The Convair 990A was distinguished from other four-engine jets by the four 'speed pods' on the wing trailing edge

delivered. Swissair took delivery of the first aircraft, HB-ICA *Bern*, on 12 January 1962 and became the first airline in the world to put the new type into service at the end of February.

A growth version of the 880, the 990-30A-6, built by the Convair Division of General Dynamics, differed principally in a lengthened fuselage to increase maximum capacity to 134 passengers, a larger wing with four anti-shock bodies on the trailing edge to allow a higher cruising speed for a given engine thrust setting, increased fuel capacity, and four 71.4 kN (16,050 lb) General Electric CJ-805-23B turbofan engines. The 990A still holds the record of the world's fastest subsonic commercial airliner, with a maximum speed in level flight of Mach 0.97, equivalent to a true airspeed of 1,067 km/h. All were later modified to improve performance, with changes comprising a fairing on the leading edge of the outer engine pylons; fairings on the inner face of all four pylons to slow down the airflow over the pylon-wing intersection; longer, less sharply tapered fairings over the engine thrust reversers; and a recontoured leading edge with no slats, but with Krüger flaps over the whole span. All Coronados of Swissair and SAS had been completed by the end of 1964.

Swissair later acquired an eighth aircraft and used the type on long-haul routes to South America, West Africa, and the Middle and Far East, with 100 passengers including 16 first class, before relegating them to European routes

Comfortable lounge on the Convair 990A

with heavy traffic, configured for 120 passengers. All left the fleet in 1975, with HB-ICE *Vaud* operating the last flight to Nice on 6 January. Some were sold to Spanish airline Spantax. After being retired, HB-ICC was donated to the *Verkehrshaus* (Swiss Transport Museum) at Lucerne, where it remains on display.

Unfortunately, HB-ICD had come to a sad end when it crashed near Würenlingen after take-off from Zurich/Kloten on 21 February 1970, with the loss of all 47 people on board. Seven minutes after take-off, an explosion occurred in the cargo hold, pressurisation was lost, and a fire and smoke prevented the crew from seeing their instruments. The

Hostesses on a course posing in front of the Convair 990A HB-ICF *Schaffhausen*

aircraft entered a steep descent and impacted the wooded Unterwald area some 24 km north-west of the airport. The Popular Front for the Liberation of Palestine (PFLP) was blamed for the attack, but no one was ever brought to justice. This bombing, and another that same day on an Austrian Airlines Caravelle, led to a 1971 UN treaty, named the *Convention for the Suppression of Unlawful Acts against the Safety of Civil Aviation*.

A new twice-weekly Zurich-Montreal-Chicago service was added to the North Atlantic routes on 17 May 1962, while, as a result of the refusal of the Brazilian Government for Swissair to continue serving São Paulo, the airline added an extension to Santiago de Chile on 26 August. The introduction of the Convair 990A Coronado, replacing the DC-6B, provided increased benefits on the South Atlantic routes. Services to the Middle East were affected by tensions in the region, which forced the cessation of the Damascus service, although some re-routing made it possible to serve Khartoum and Dhahran once again. On 1 April, Swissair was also able to resume its service to Abadan in Iran. West Africa received a new weekly service on 2 May 1962 to Accra and Lagos via Tripoli, although the stop at Tripoli was soon eliminated. Changes to the European network included new direct services from Zurich to Barcelona, Palma de Mallorca and Hamburg; from Geneva to Copenhagen; and from Basle to Munich and Geneva.

Time for consolidation

The following year was a time for consolidation, with Zurich-Geneva-Algiers, opened on 6 July 1963, and Geneva-Milan the only new routes added to the network. A fourth DC-8, a turbofan-powered DC-8-53, HB-IDD *Nidwalden*, was added in October, and three DC-3 remained for training flights and some internal services and special freight flights. A tragedy, the worst in Swissair's history, was the crash of the Caravelle III, HB-ICV *Schaffhausen*, on 4 September 1963,

with the loss of six crew and 74 passengers. What made the disaster particularly devastating was that 43 of the dead came from the small Swiss village of Humlikon, leaving behind the young and elderly. The Caravelle was on a flight from Zurich/Kloten to Rome, with an intermediate stop at Geneva/Cointrin. Only minutes after take-off in dense fog from Zurich, the aircraft, trailing a long flame, began to lose height and finally went into a steep dive. Parts of the aircraft became detached and it crashed into the ground on the outskirts of Dürrenäsch, some 35 km from Zurich. The crash was traced to the destruction of essential structural parts of the aircraft by a fire caused by overheating of the brakes during the taxiing phase.

Swissair had been mulling over the replacement of the Convair 440 Metropolitan for some time, as the small piston-engined aircraft was no longer able to match the competition from newer aircraft introduced by other airlines in Europe. After lengthy studies and discussions with several aircraft manufacturers, Swissair came to the conclusion that the Douglas DC-9 would best meet the demands of its short-haul network and it was agreed on 13 May 1964 to place an order for 15 DC-9-15 twinjets, adding two more later that year. Deliveries were to take place from 1966, in a phased programme to ensure the availability of adequate numbers of pilots and the establishment of necessary technical infrastructure. A DC-9 simulator was ordered at the end of the year. The only new route in 1964 was the Zurich-Geneva-Tunis-Tripoli line, inaugurated on 6 July, which was operated with Swissair's own aircraft from 1 November, having previously leased a Caravelle from Tunis Air for the Geneva-Tunis sector. A Caravelle III, HB-ICR, was also leased from Air France between 28 February 1964 and 4 March 1966. On 17 April 1964, a capital increase to CHF 140 million was approved.

Swissair came under increasing criticism for neglecting to establish an internal network, and especially for not

The turbo-fan powered Douglas DC-8-53 HB-IDD *Nidwalden*

Fokker F.27-400 Friendship operated by Balair for Swissair on new domestic routes

connecting the capital Berne into its international services. The airline accepted that as the national carrier, it had a responsibility to bring into its system those regional cities were an actual or potential commercial demand existed, but had to balance this against the need to ensure its own economic viability. The airport at Bern/Belpmoos was too small for its existing aircraft fleet, and Swissair acquired a single Fokker F.27-400 Friendship twin-turboprop aircraft, HB-AAV, to provide a connection between Berne and Zurich. This was operated by Basle-based Balair and, after some improvements at Berne, went into service on 11 June 1965. Basle was also brought into the network. Two more Friendships were ordered in March and December 1966, also operated by Balair. The European network was enhanced with new services to Budapest and Zagreb, while a new route was opened in Africa, serving Abidjan and Monrovia from 3 April 1965, and the Algiers line was extended to Casablanca. An agreement was signed with

KLM under which Swissair would maintain the engines of the incoming DC-9 aircraft for both companies, while KLM was to carry out the same work on the turbofan engines of the DC-8 fleet.

Having re-assessed its requirement for the Convair 440 replacement and the growing demand in Europe, Swissair came to the conclusion that the DC-9-15 would be too small and changed a part of the order on 6 July 1967 to the larger DC-9-32, which Douglas was developing to meet the competition from the Boeing 737 twinjet. Providing seating for 95 passengers, compared to the 75 in the DC-9-15, a 50 per cent increase in underfloor capacity, and more powerful Pratt & Whitney JT8D turbofan engines, the DC-9-32 also featured high-lift devices including full span leading-edge slats and triple-slotted flaps for improved take-off and landing performance. It also promised a maximum speed of 897 km/h and a typical range of 2,800 km. The first DC-9-15, HB-IFA *Graubünden*, was delivered

Douglas DC-9-15 HB-IFA *Graubünden* and DC-9-32 HB-IFF *Fribourg* at Geneva

Douglas DC-9-32 close to touchdown

via the Azores on 20 July 1966 and entered service on the route from Zurich and Basle to London in August. Two more arrived at Zurich before the end of the year, with another two in 1967. Apart from London, the DC-9 was also quickly scheduled on the services to Barcelona, Palma, Brussels, Paris, Munich and Milan.

On 1 January 1967, the *Eidgenössische Verkehrs- und Energiewirtschaftsdepartement* (Federal Department for Transport and Economy), granted Swissair a concession for 15 years, confirming its status as the national airline. While until 1967, all Swissair share capital was in registered shares, which could be held only by Swiss citizens, new bearer shares could now also be bought by foreigners. The statutes were changed to enshrine in law that bearer shares were at no time to account for more than one-third of the share capital.

Recessions in various European countries, renewed conflicts in the Middle East and crises in Greece, Cyprus,

Nigeria and Hong Kong, impacted the airline's performance in the first half of the year, although the year-end result was still satisfactory. Due to the slow delivery of the Douglas DC-9-32, the first of which, HB-IFF *Fribourg* did not arrive until 21 October 1967, Swissair wet-leased a BAC 1-11-200, G-ATVH, twinjet from British Eagle between 1 April and 14 November 1967, replaced by a 1-11-300, G-ATPK, the following day and operated until 29 April 1968. The two McDonnell Douglas DC-8-62, HB-IDE *Genève* and HB-IDF *Zürich*, ordered to replace the two early turbojet-powered DC-8-32, were also delayed and did not arrive until 23 November 1967 and 2 January 1968 respectively. Swissair had hoped to put the new larger aircraft onto the North Atlantic services much earlier in the year, as more capacity was needed. Orders were placed for three additional DC-9-32 and two more DC-8-62, one of which was for the DC-8-62CF Combi passenger/cargo version. The medium- and long-haul routes were little

Mcdonnell Douglas DC-8-62 HB-IDE *Genève* at a snowy Zurich

The McDonnell Douglas DC-8-62CF was a convertible passenger/cargo aircraft

changed in the year, but the European network was further expanded with new services to Bucharest, Helsinki, Malaga and Moscow. Berne was linked to Paris, served by Balair with the F.27 on behalf of Swissair.

All-jet operation

With the last flight of the Convair 440 Metropolitan completed on 31 October 1968, Swissair became an all-jet operator, one of the earliest airlines in the world. Two more DC-8-62 and 13 DC-9-32 were delivered in the year, the latter eventually numbering 20 aircraft, including a single DC-9-33F freighter, HB-IFW *Payerne*. At the same time, the five smaller DC-9-15 aircraft were returned to McDonnell Douglas. The African network was enlarged with new services to Nairobi, Dar-es-Salaam and Johannesburg on 1 April. Other significant developments in 1968 were the renewal of the agreement with SAS for another 10 years, and discussions for closer co-operation

with its neighbour Austrian Airlines. The co-operation agreement with SAS was extended on 13 January 1969 to include KLM Royal Dutch Airlines and became known as the KSS Group. A year later, French carrier UTA was added, resulting in the official establishment of the KSSU Consortium on 18 February 1970. Negotiations were initiated with Austrian Airlines with a view of creating a joint airline, similar to the Scandinavian Airlines System. It was suggested that Austrian would take a financial stake and have two management positions, with the expanded operation given the preliminary name of Swissair-Austrian. However, the plan foundered, its failure attributed to unsolvable legal issues regarding the share distribution, fear of losing national identity, and last but not least through the intervention of the British Government, which saw its projected sale of the BAC One-Eleven jet endangered. Instead, the two airlines agreed on a closer technical and operational co-operation.

The BAC-111-200 G-ATVH was leased briefly due to the late delivery of the Douglas DC-9-32

In spite of the increased seat capacity, Swissair ended the year in a satisfactory position, achieved largely through a substantial increase in freight traffic. This was further consolidated in 1969, when Swissair, for the first time, achieved revenues in excess of CFH 1,000 million. With a recognisable move towards mass tourism, increased costs set against the continuing downward pressure on prices, convinced Swissair that the future lay in the emergence of large-capacity wide-body aircraft. Already on 28 April 1967, the Board had authorised an order for two four-engined Boeing 747-200B, and now followed this move with an order in June 1969 for six McDonnell Douglas DC-10-30 trijets, which not only provided seating for 250 passengers, but also offered greatly-increased space for freight. Options were also placed for five more, all of which were taken up. Financing of these new aircraft was to be eased with a capital increase to around CHF 300 million and long credit from the capital market. A further increase to CHF 335 million was completed the following year. New services were opened to Colombo and Singapore, but the Zurich-Frankfurt-New York route had to be closed on 1 November 1969, with Swissair improving the flights to Montreal and Chicago. New daily flights in Europe were started to Rotterdam and Manchester. The only new routes in 1970 were to Oslo as an extension to the Copenhagen service, Douala and Kinshasa, all opened on 1 April, but the Berne-Paris service had to be discontinued for lack of demand.

Swissair's first wide-body aircraft, the Boeing 747-200B, HB-IGA *Genève*, was delivered on 29 January 1971, followed by the second, HB-IGB *Zürich*, on 25 March. Both entered service on the New York service on 1 April, replacing the DC-8, and by August were providing 12 roundtrips a week. Swissair placed further orders for the 747-200B, but with stretched upper deck (SUD), but these were later changed to the improved 747-300. The Swissair aircraft were powered by the Pratt & Whitney JT9D turbofan engines, and had a speed of 939 km/h and a range of 12.500 km. Accommodation was provided for 32 passengers in first-class and 329 in economy, and the aircraft could also carry 10 tonnes of freight in its belly-hold. The appreciation of the Swiss franc on 9 May 1971 hit Swissair hard and resulted in a loss of income of CHF 42 million. Another negative event was a ban on night flights at Zurich, Geneva and Basle, implemented on 1 November 1972. Particularly affected by this decision were Swissair's European freight flights and the popular last evening flights from London. However, the six-hour ban was timed to allow the scheduled departures at Geneva for South America and South Africa. The first McDonnell Douglas DC-10-30, HB-IHA *St Gallen*, was delivered on 30 November 1972, Swissair becoming the first airline to operate the type over water, flying a Zurich-Montreal-Chicago service on 15 December.

Desert drama

In September 1970, members of the Popular Front for the Liberation of Palestine (PFLP) hijacked four airliners bound for New York, and one for London, one of which was Swissair Flight 100 from Zurich, operated with a Douglas DC-8-53, HB-IDD Nidwalden. On board were 12 crew and 143 passengers. The aircraft was seized over Paris on 6 September by a male and a female, one of them having a silver revolver. An announcement over the intercom informed the passengers that the aircraft had been taken over by the PFLP and that it was being diverted to Dawson's Field, a remote and disused desert airstrip near Zarqa, Jordan, formerly the UK Royal Air Force Station Zerqa, which then became the PFLP's Matar ath-Thawra (revolution airport). Also diverted to Dawson's Field were a TWA Boeing 707 registered N8715T, which was on a round-the-world flight with 144 passengers and 11 crew, and a BOAC Vickers VC-10, G-ASGN flying from Bombay to London via Bahrain and Beirut, which was hijacked after departing Bahrain About 125 hostages were taken to Amman and other locations, while the American, Israeli, Swiss and German citizens were held on the aircraft. On 7 September, the hijackers held a press conference for the world's media, demanding the release of several Palestinian and Arab prisoners held in jails in Israel and other European countries. Passengers were released in trickles, except the hijackers held on to 54 hostages, most of them Jewish and American men, in secret hide-outs in Amman. On 12 September, all three, then empty aircraft, were blown up and completely destroyed. The last hostages were released in exchange for Leila Khaled, which had been handed over to the British Government after a foiled hijack of an El AL Boeing 707 at Amsterdam, and three that were held in Switzerland.

Swissair's first Boeing 747-200B HB-IGA was delivered on 29 January 1971

McDonnell Douglas produced the wide-body DC-10 as a successor to the DC-8 for the long-range market. The DC-10-30 was powered by three General Electric CF6-50 two-shaft, high bypass ratio turbofan engines, two on underwing pylons and a third at the base of the vertical stabiliser, and had increased fuel capacity over earlier models, to provide an intercontinental range of 9,600 km and improved fuel efficiency. It was fitted with a ground proximity warning system (GPWS), which gave aural and visual warnings of imminent inadvertent contact with the ground. Swissair configured the DC-10 for 237 passengers in two classes. In July 1980, Swissair became the launch customer for the extended-range DC-10-30ER, taking delivery of two aircraft, HB-IHN *St Gallen* on 27 February and HB-IHO *Uri*, on 1 April 1982. Later that year, two earlier aircraft, HB-IHL *Thurgau* and HB-IHM *Wallis*, were converted to DC-10-30ER standard. The DC-10-30ER had a higher maximum take-off weight, more powerful 240 kN (54,000 lb) CF6-50C2B engines, and was equipped with an additional fuel tank in the rear cargo hold to extend the range by 1,125 km.

Oil shock

In October 1973, members of the Organization of Arab Petroleum Exporting Countries (OAPEC) proclaimed an oil embargo. Although this was initially targeted at nations perceived as supporting Israel during the Yom Kippur War that same month, its effect was felt throughout the world. By the end of the embargo, oil prices had risen nearly 300 per cent. Swissair had to reduce or reschedule its long-haul services and, for safety reasons had to temporarily cancel its flights to the Middle East. But these events, and the ongoing currency crisis, were not the only ones that affected operations. Lengthy conflicts of air traffic controllers in France and Germany forced Swissair to cancel or re-route flights, which led to the inevitable delays. Elsewhere, the terrorist attacks and hijackings at Rome's Leonardo da Vinci-Fiumicino International Airport also depressed demand for air travel. Not surprisingly, there were no additions to the network during the year, and only Marseille was added in 1974, when the uncertainty of fuel supplies still dogged the airline.

With an eye on the future, however, Swissair had originated the requirement for the higher-capacity DC-9-51 twin-jet with an order for 10 aircraft, ordering two more in 1977. With a fuselage stretch of 4.36 m over

McDonnell Douglas DC-10-30 HB-IGA *St Gallen* was Swissair's first in a fleet that eventually numbered 15 aircraft including two DC-10-30ER

McDonnell Douglas DC-9-51 HB-ISM named *Wettingen*

McDonnell Douglas DC-9-41 HB-IDW, ex OY-KGA of Scandinavian Airlines System (SAS)

McDonnell Douglas MD-81 in new Swissair livery on the taxiway at Zurich/Kloten

the DC-9-32, the DC-9-51 provided accommodation for 120 passengers, and had more powerful 71.2 kN (16,000 lb) JT8D-17 turbofan engines. It also incorporated detailed improvements but was visually little different to earlier models, with the exception of small strakes below the side cockpit windows, spray deflectors on the nose gear, and inward angled thrust reversers. While awaiting the delivery of the new aircraft, Swissair leased four DC-9-41 from SAS in late 1974, a version, which fitted in size between the DC-9-32 and DC-9-51 and had been specially developed for the Scandinavian airline.

While the first half of 1975 was still affected by currency problems and persistent depression of tariffs, the second half witnessed an upturn in traffic and enabled Swissair to once again extend its network. New services were added to Beijing and Shanghai on 6 April, to ensure a foothold in China's growing participation in the world economy, and a relative calm in the Middle East, encouraged Swissair to add Dhahran and Abu Dhabi to the schedule. The continued weakness of the US dollar affected North American traffic, although a new service was opened to Toronto. A deterioration in Europe's economy particularly impacted the services to Eastern Europe, Germany and Spain. The first DC-9-51, HB-ISM *Wettingen*, entered service on 24 August 1975. By the end of the year, five DC-9-51 were in

service, and more DC-10-30 deliveries brought the total in the fleet to eight. Terminal B was opened at Zurich/Kloten, doubling the airport's handling capacity to 12 million. The improvement in the latter part of the year was continued into 1976, with a 12.8 per cent increase in traffic, and enabled Swissair to strengthen its network with new services to Oran in Algeria, Dubai and Kuwait in the Middle East.

Passenger traffic continued its upward movement and was even exceeded by the cargo business, which had been in the doldrums for some time. Linz, Sofia and Ankara were added to the schedule, and frequencies were increased on the Geneva-Zurich link. The airline's capital was increased to CHF 448 million. At the instigation of Swissair with a launch order on 19 October 1977 for 15 DC-9-81, later redesignated MD-81, plus five options, McDonnell Douglas proceeded with this mid-size, medium-range growth version of the DC-9-51. With a larger wing providing extra fuel capacity, and 4.3 m longer, the MD-81 offered seating for up to 155 passengers, although carrying only 134 passengers in Swissair service, and a maximum payload range of 3,300 km. It was powered by the higher bypass Pratt & Whitney JT8D-200 turbofan engines, generating a thrust of 82.3 kN (18,500 lb). Also featured were cockpit, avionics and aerodynamics upgrades, including a digital electronics integrated flight guidance and control system, Autoland, a 'dial a flap' system for optimum take-off performance, a larger capacity auxiliary power unit (APU), and an advanced digital fuel quantity gauging system. Swissair took delivery of its first aircraft, HB-INC *Thurgau*, on 12 September 1980, which entered service on 5 October with a Zurich-Frankfurt roundtrip.

The Airline Deregulation Act in the United States in 1978, which created a free market, set in motion a price war on the North Atlantic, which depressed income in spite of an increase in passenger numbers. Currency problems also continued to plague the airline. No great developments were recorded in the network, with only Oporto, Jeddah, and Annaba (Algeria) added. However, Swissair decided to change its ageing corporate identity. The arrow logo was abandoned and replaced with new black lettering in lower case and prominent dots on the i, with the national emblem of the white cross in a red field in rhomboid form alongside. The tail units of the aircraft were unchanged, and the red windowline was retained, until replaced by a two-tone cheatline in chocolate brown below the windows in 1981. At the same time, the Swissair lettering was changed to red, and the national flag was extended to cover the whole of the tailfin.

Significant setbacks were suffered in 1979, first with the 12-day grounding of the entire DC-10-30 fleet, following a crash of an American Airlines DC-10 at Chicago on 25 May, and on 7 October, when its DC-8-62, HB-IDE *Uri*, overshot the wet runway at Athens/Ellinikon International and burst into flames killing 14 of the 142 passengers on board. The crew of 12 survived. The accident investigation determined that the crew touched down too far along the runway, at too high a speed, following a non-stabilised approach. The aircraft came to rest on a public road, where the wing and tail separated and a fire broke out. Both pilots were charged and found guilty of manslaughter and negligence in failing to properly utilise the aircraft's brake and reverse thrust system. A marked effect on costs was the persistently high oil price, which had doubled by the end of the year. On the positive side, as a joint launch customer with Lufthansa, Swissair became the first airline to place an order for the new Airbus A310-200, when it signed up for 10 plus 10 options, on 15 March 1979. It also ordered a third Boeing 747-200B in December, and optioned one more. Dublin was the only city added to the network.

Flightdeck of the McDonnell Douglas MD-81

Steady progress

In a year, which IATA described as the worst ever in the history of air transport, Swissair emerged from 1980 with a loss, the first since 1975, but proclaimed itself satisfied with its overall performance. With high oil prices, which rose by 62 per cent in the year, still increasing costs, Swissair continued to invest in new fuel-efficient aircraft. The first three McDonnell Douglas MD-81 twinjets, which eventually reached 26 aircraft, arrived during the year and went on to form the flagship of the short-medium haul network. An order was also placed on 11 June 1980 for four new Boeing 747-300 with the Stretched Upper Deck (SUD), and also converted the outstanding order to the new type. At the same time, the airline also signed up for two extended-range McDonnell Douglas DC-10 trijets, while also converting two earlier models to the ER variant. Minimal changes to the route system included the addition of the Indonesian capital Jakarta, but the outbreak of the Iran/Iraq war on 22 September 1980, which turned into prolonged military conflict, forced Swissair to cease flying to Tehran and Baghdad. As an alternative, it provided surface transport to the two cities from Amman in Jordan, and from the Turkish capital Ankara. Of note was the inclusion of Zurich/Kloten into the national network of the *Schweizerische Bundesbahnen-SBB* (Swiss Federal Railways), which enabled the elimination of bus transport to the airport from the city centre. At the same time, in co-operation with the SBB, Swissair introduced the '*Fly-Gepäck*' service, which enabled passengers to hand in their luggage at the

railway station and travel unhindered to Zurich/Kloten and Geneva/Cointrin. Already 72 railways station could be included in this innovative service.

In spite of the continued negative performance of the world's air transport, Swissair was able to hold its own and still managed to achieve modest profits. Revenues exceeded CHF 3 billion for the first time in 1981. A five-year commercial agreement was signed with the fast-growing regional airline Crossair, under which Swissair handed over some of its minor routes. Deliveries of the DC-9-81 were completed in 1982, and the two DC-10-30ER, HB-IHN *St Gallen* and HB-IHO *Uri*, were delivered that same year. The introduction of the new aircraft, and the new destinations of Thessaloniki, Greece and Harare, Zimbabwe, enabled Swissair to increase its offer by 5 per cent. The services to Baghdad and Tehran could also be re-activated.

The fleet underwent a major change in 1983, with the DC-8 and 747-200B taken out of service, along with some DC-9 and early DC-10 aircraft, and the delivery of the first three of five wide-body Airbus A310-200 twin-engined, and four Boeing 747-300, two of which were of the Combi passenger/freight version. The first A310-200, HB-IPA *Aargau*, was delivered on 25 March 1983 and operated its first revenue flight on 21 April. It was powered by two 213.5 kN (48,000 lb) Pratt & Whitney JT9D-7R4 turbofan engines, had a cruising speed of 850 km/h, a range of 6,500 km, and provided typical two-class accommodation for 212 passengers. The flightdeck was designed with the aid of stylists from the Porsche luxury car manufacturer, to

Boeing 747-300 HB-IGD *Basel* flying over the Grand Combin massif, which exceeds 4,000 m in height

Airbus A310-200 HB-IPD *Solothurn* flying past the Weisshorn mountain group

produce a spacious and ergonomically-styled interior, with crew comfort and low workload the prime considerations. From the outset, accommodation was provided for two crew members, captain and first officer. From 1985, Swissair also took delivery of five A310-300 models, with more powerful engines, additional fuel tanks for increased range of 7,200 km, and wingtip fences for improved aerodynamic efficiency. It was the first operator of the new variant. To increase the comfort of passengers on flights longer than three hours, Swissair reduced the capacity on the A310-300

to 172 passengers (22 in first-class, 61 in business, and 89 in economy).

The 747-300M was the same size as the earlier 747-200B, but minor aerodynamic changes increased the cruising speed. It had cargo capacity with six pallets on the rear portion of the main deck but, with the stretched upper deck, passenger capacity was affected little. The underfloor cargo capacity was five pallets and 4-6 LD-3 containers. The first aircraft, HB-IGD *Basel*, arrived at Zurich/Kloten on 3 March 1983. As the launch customer for both the A310

Fokker 100 HB-IVA *Aarau* taking off from Zurich

Airbus A310-300 HB-IPF *Glarus* in flight over the Rhône Valley

and B747-300, Swissair was able to secure favourable prices, and was in the fortunate position to largely self-finance these acquisitions. Few changes were made to the network, with Toulouse and Riyadh bringing the total number of destinations served to one hundred.

Swissair refitted the first class on all its long-haul aircraft with more comfortable seats, which it named slumberettes, and also introduced business class from summer 1984, flying with three classes on all flights, apparently the only airline to do so at the time. In a further modernisation of the fleet, the management board decided to order eight Fokker 100 regional jets, plus two options, and retired the last DC-8. Larnaca was the only new destinations, but the services to Annaba and Harare were discontinued. Rio de Janeiro was served non-stop for the first time. The airline's financial strength was improved with a capital increase to CHF 568 million. Caracas was added in 1985, but war clouds in the Gulf forced Swissair to serve Tehran indirectly, flying to Bandar Abbas, from where Iran Air took its passengers to

Tehran. In the following year, Swissair enlarged its network with eight new destinations, which included Anchorage over the Polar route, Ankara (re-introduced), Bahrain, Birmingham (UK), Malta, Tirana, Brazzaville and Seoul. A further injection of capital brought it to CHF 615 million. Flights at regular intervals between Zurich and Frankfurt were introduced jointly by Swissair and Lufthansa, adding to a similar arrangement between Geneva and Paris with Air France the previous year, the latter to counteract the competition from the newly-opened TGV rail service between the two cities.

Yet, the financial performance, while still considered satisfactory, was influenced by the terrorist attacks at Rome and Vienna, as well as the nuclear disaster of Chernobyl, which depressed travel in Europe. However, traffic rebounded in 1987 and produced better than expected financial results. An expression of confidence in the future was the order for 12 McDonnell Douglas MD-11 trijets, as a gradual replacement for the DC-10-30 fleet. The advantages

McDonnell Douglas MD-11 HB-IWB *Graubünden*

MD-11 HB-IWN of Swissair Asia at Zurich/Kloten

Swissair Asia MD-11 with the Chinese-character rui meaning Switzerland on the tailfin, which eased its services to Taipei and Shanghai were stated to be the increased range, which was expected to reach Hong Kong non-stop with a full payload, and extend as far as Tokyo over the trans-Siberian route. Relatively quiet engines and good fuel economy were also attractive. The MD-11 purchase required an investment of CHF 2 billion. Another important decision was its participation with British Airways and KLM in the European Galileo reservation system, which was consolidated with Swissair joining the American COVIA system in 1988, with a 11.3 per cent stake. Also welcome was a decision by the European Civil Aviation Conference (ECAC) on 1 January 1987, which created more flexibility in intra-European air transport with regards to frequencies, size of aircraft and setting tariffs. Some streamlining of the network was implemented. Apart from the new services to Atlanta and Turin, Swissair stopped serving Santiago de Chile, Colombo, Bahrain and Dublin for economic reasons, and those to Dhahran and Oran due to traffic right problems.

All-weather operation

The delivery of the eight Fokker 100 and three more MD-81, and the removal of the last four DC-9-51 and three DC-9-32 twinjets, brought the average fleet age to just 5.7 years. Furthermore, the entire fleet was now CAT IIIA-compliant, permitting automatic landing in extreme weather conditions. Swissair was the first airline to be so equipped throughout its entire fleet. The first Fokker 100, HB-IVA *Aarau*, was delivered on 1 March 1988, and the last of the eight orders arrived at Zurich on 21 November that year. The two options were also taken up and delivered in April 1992. The Fokker 100 regional jet was based on the earlier F.28-4000 Fellowship, with a fuselage stretched by 5.74m to seat up to 109 passengers, although it carried only 84 passengers in Swissair service. It was re-engined with two newer and quieter 61.6 kN (13,850 lb) Rolls-Royce Tay Mk 620-15 high bypass-ratio turbofans and had an updated glass cockpit and a wider wing and tail for increased maximum weights. Fuel economy was also improved by 20 per cent over previous generation aircraft. Minimal changes were made to the schedule, with Graz, Bordeaux and Catania added, and Khartoum withdrawn. Check-in possibilities were enlarged, with its introduction at major Swiss railway stations.

The co-operation with regional airline Crossair, which had been in place since 1982, was strengthened with Swissair taking a 38.3 per cent stake in the airline. The wide-ranging and close relationship with Austrian Airlines was also consolidated with a 3 per cent stake, soon

McDonnell Douglas DC-10-30 HB-IHB *Schaffhausen* and HB-IHD *Bern*

Airbus A321-100 HB-IOH with additional Qualifyer markings

increased to 10 per cent. Further collaborative agreements were concluded with Delta Air Lines on 16 March 1989, followed by SAS on 28 September and Singapore Airlines (SIA) on 14 December that same year, known as *Global Excellence*, with the aim of creating lasting competitiveness and promoting the expansion of quality global services, while preserving Swissair's independence. An Extraordinary General Assembly of shareholders voted on 12 September to increase the share capital to CHF 709 million, to allow a 5.9 per cent cross-equity investment with Delta. In 1991, Swissair and Singapore Airlines completed a cross-equity arrangement, whereby Swissair acquired 0.62 per cent of SIA, while SIA obtained a 2.77 per cent holding in Swissair.

After years of tough negotiations, Swissair finally managed to get access to the West Coast of America, inaugurating a service to Los Angeles, California on 1 November 1989. Several more additions to the network were made to Lyon on 27 March, to Izmir and Ljubljana on 28 March, and on 29 October to Gothenburg. On 28 June, a DC-10-30ER made the first non-stop flight to Tokyo across Siberia in 11 hours 54 minutes. Santiago de Chile was served once again, with the connecting flight from Buenos Aires flown by Chilean airline Ladeco. The withdrawal of the freight flight to Glasgow on 26 July meant the end of all-cargo operations. From then on, freight was carried exclusively in the belly hold of its passenger aircraft. The year 1990 was marked

The *Quali*flyer Group

The name Qualiflyer was created in April 1992 as Europe's first frequent flyer programme (FFP) of Swissair, Crossair and Austrian Airlines, later joined by other European carriers. When Swissair bought up minority stakes in several airlines, co-operation was strengthened with the establishment of the Qualiflyer Group in 1998. At the height of its existence, the alliance members served 332 destinations worldwide with 469 aircraft, carrying close to 50 million passengers annually. Members included Swissair, Crossair, Sabena, Air Littoral, AOM French Airlines, Air Europe, LOT, Portugalia, TAP Air Portugal, and Volare Airlines. LTU and Turkish Airlines were not full members but participated in the FFP. With the collapse of Swissair, the Qualiflyer Group was dissolved in 2002, although the FFP continued to exist for a short time, until the airlines started their own programmes, or joined existing ones.

by the Gulf War and its aftermath, a weak economy and rising insurance and petrol costs, which resulted in a loss in Swissair's air transport operation, although this was made up of income from third-party work and other interests, leaving a small net profit. Together with SAS, Austrian Airlines and Finnair, Swissair formed the *European Quality Alliance,* later transformed into the Qualiflyer Alliance. Additions to the network were Bilbao, Valencia and Philadelphia and, for the first time since 1947, Swissair was once again able to serve Berlin. Services to Catania, Amman, Kuwait, Baghdad and Monrovia were discontinued for economic or political reasons. A major decision was made by the Board to place an order with Airbus for 26 A320/321 twin-engined aircraft, plus options for 26 more, to replace its MD-81 fleet on the European network.

The Gulf War, which finally ended on 28 February 1991, affected the schedule at the beginning of the year. All services to Abu Dhabi, Damascus, Dubai, Jeddah, Riyadh and Tel Aviv had to be suspended between 5 January and 17 March. Changes to the network during the year included a joint service with Austrian Airlines to Kiev and St Petersburg on 31 March, and a new service to Delhi on 24 June, with the first non-stop service from Zurich to Beijing opened that same day. Other non-stop flights were inaugurated to Johannesburg on 27 October, and to Hong Kong on 30 October. On the negative side, services were discontinued to Ljubljana, Zagreb and Kinshasa due to political tensions in Yugoslavia and Zaïre, while stops at Anchorage and Jakarta were removed with the introduction of non-stop flights to destinations further afield.

The first McDonnell Douglas MD-11, HB-IWA *Obwalden*, arrived in Switzerland on 7 March 1991 and entered service on 21 March. Powered by three 280 kN (62,000 lb) Pratt & Whitney PW4460 turbofan engines in a similar arrangement to the DC-10, the MD-11 offered a range of 12,450 km and was configured in Swissair service with 257 seats in a three-class layout. Of the nine aircraft delivered in 1991, five were acquired on a lease basis. Swissair prided itself on its measured and carefully evaluated decisions regarding the development of its fleet, but the choice of the MD-11 was perhaps the least sensible, as the era of the three/four-engined aircraft was being supplanted by new long-range twinjets and the advent of extended twin operations (ETOPS) over water and remote lands.

In a referendum on 6 December 1992, Switzerland narrowly rejected joining the European Economic Area (EAA), which was detrimental to Swissair's ability to compete effectively against its competitors in the internal market, preventing it from operating direct connections between EEA member countries, nor pick up passengers on intermediate stops. Set against this were increased synergies achieved with its partners Delta, Singapore and Austrian, and other measures to relieve the pressure on the bottom line included the transfer of all flights in and out of Basle to Crossair, and moves towards a fusion of Balair and CTA to secure their competitiveness in the charter market. Both companies agreed to a merger on 18/19 May 1993, which was implemented retroactively on 1 January, with Swissair increasing its holding to 94 per cent at the same time. Additions to the passenger schedule were new services to Vilnius on 19 January 1992, Washington DC on 14 September, and Minsk, Banjul and Yaounde on 25 October. Political events again forced a suspension of flights to Tripoli and Belgrade, although Swissair was able

Airbus A321-100 HB-IOA

to re-introduce flights to Ljubljana, Zagreb and Kinshasa. On 31 May, the DC-10-30 operated its final service, and the delivery of the twelfth MD-11 on 3 June completed the transfer to the new trijet.

Better together?

Swissair, as other national airlines in smaller countries, came under increasing pressure to follow the growing trend towards airline alliances, to create economies of scale to better compete in the global world. On 6 November 1993, the management of Swissair, SAS, KLM and Austrian Airlines announced in Stockholm that they had agreed to merge their airlines under the name of

Onboard service in business class on the Airbus A321-100

Symphony and were about to sign on the dotted line. The top-secret *Project Alcázar* had been in the making since 27 January and was the last in a long line of attempts to create a conglomerate that would have been a major force in Europe. but it underestimated the problems that had to be overcome, not least how to value each carrier in terms of participation. It had been intended to allocate a 30 per cent share to Swissair, SAS and KLM, and 10 per cent to Austrian Airlines. Each carrier also operated different

aircraft, there were two types of computer reservation systems, seemingly insurmountable issues with the labour unions, and discussions on whether the headquarters were to be located at Copenhagen or Amsterdam. Even a suggestion that each airline would retain its own aircraft and hire its own flight and technical crew, and the merged carrier thus becoming a virtual airline, failed to overcome the challenges posed. While SAS was willing to relinquish its stake in Continental Airlines, neither Swissair nor KLM

Airbus A320-200 with provisional French registration F-WWIF bedore becoming HB-IJA *Opfikon*

Airbus A320-200 HB-IPF *Rümlang*

were prepared to abandon their American partners and, when on 21 November, KLM pulled out, the project fell apart. At the end of the year, Swissair instead initiated negotiations with Belgian airline Sabena.

Of note were the introduction of business-class instead of first-class on short-haul routes, as well as new services to Harare and Cape Town on 29 June, and to Muscat on 6 November. The only addition to the network in 1994, was the service to Osaka, inaugurated on 4 September. The Board decided in March 1995, to transfer the long-range element of BalairCTA to Swissair, and the short-range business to Crossair. All schedules with aircraft of less than 100 seats were also handed over to Crossair, which helped not only to reduce the fleet composition, but also costs and duplication of services. Balair/CTA ceased all operations on 31 October 1995, but was resurrected as a long-haul charter subsidiary in 1997 under the name of Balair/CTA Leisure AG.

On 7 April, Swissair opened a twice-weekly service to Taipei, Taiwan (Republic of China), which was flown under the name of Swissair Asia, to safeguard its traffic rights to the Democratic People's Republic of China. Three MD-11, HB-IWG *Valais/Wallis*, HB-IWL *Appenzell Ausserrhoden* and HB-IWN, were operated in a different livery, where the Swiss Cross on the tailfin was replaced by the Chinese character *rui*, from the Chinese translation of Switzerland, set in white into a red tail. This ruse enabled the re-instatement of the service to Shanghai on 4 November. Singapore received non-stop flights, and joint Swissair/Austrian/ Delta services were opened over the route Vienna-Geneva-Washington on 26 March, followed by a Swissair/Austrian

service to Almaty on 30 March. The delivery of the first Airbus A321-100, HB-IOC, on 25 January 1995, and of the first A320-200, HB-IJA *Opfikon*, on 31 May, signalled the beginning of the next phase of the short/medium-haul fleet renewal. Swissair specified the CFM International CFM56-5B high-bypass turbofan engine with double-annular combustor, which reduced NOx emissions by 40 per cent compared to the MD-81. However, emissions and performance from the engine did not initially meet the promise of the manufacturer, which prompted Swissair in Spring 1997 to re-engine some aircraft with conventional CFM56 engines, although it reverted to the original engine once the performance guaranties were reached.

No progress was made in the bilateral negotiations with the European Union, ensuring the continued isolation of Switzerland and the handicapped market access combined with discriminatory tariffs. In contrast, the *Open Sky* agreement with the United States on 13 February 1995 gave Swissair unfettered access to the American market, further improved with the granting of anti-trust immunity to Swissair and Delta on 17 June 1996. All services across the North Atlantic were henceforth operated on a joint basis between Swissair and Delta, with Austrian and Sabena added within the framework of the *Atlantic Alliance* on February 1997. Income was shared among the four airlines at an agreed ratio.

In a far-reaching decision, which ultimately contributed to the downfall of both airlines, Swissair had agreed on a closer co-operation with loss-making Sabena and acquired a 49.5 per cent stake in the Belgian airline for CHF 260

The three short/medium Airbus types, A319, A320 and A321

million on 4 May 1995. This was given the green light by the EU on 19 July, but at the same time, Swissair was forced by the EU to cease its co-operative agreements with SAS. Under the agreement with Swissair, the capital of Sabena was to be increased to BEF 25.6 billion, and Swissair could increase its stake in the future to 67.7 per cent through the exercising of rights linked to warrants granted to Swissair in exchange for a loan of BEF 4 billion it had given to the Belgian Federal Investment Company with a view of taking over Finacta's stake. However, the Belgian State reserved the right to buy back the shares of the Swiss group, if its interests were seriously threatened. For Swissair, the flag-carrier of a similarly small country, outside the European Union with no home market, the collaboration with Sabena had great advantages, including access to the EU transport market, from which it had felt isolated, and Africa, a market in which Swissair was only minimally present. The advantages, other than ensuring survival, and creating economies of scale, were less clear-cut for Sabena.

Corporate reshuffle

As a precursor to a holding structure with company-protected but independent units, operations were divided into four areas of activity on 1 March 1996. The key advantages of the new structure were summarised as providing trade-specific order under overall corporate responsibility, transparency in qualitative and quantitative terms, flexible room for manoeuvre, and optimal exploitation of synergy

potentials. Flying activities of Swissair, Crossair, Balair/CTA and the co-operation with partner airlines were combined under SAirLines. Aircraft maintenance, flight handling, information technology and real estate management formed part of SAirServices, while the SAirLogistic division was made responsible for freight sales and handling, as well as warehouse management and the offer of global logistics solutions to customers. The fourth unit, SAirRelations, handled hotel management, catering and duty free. Each division was supposed to be autonomous, responsible for its own financial results, and development of its own business strategies, but all activities throughout the four divisions were defined as part of the *Swissair Experience*, and had "to pay due regard to the interest of the group as a whole". Inter-group services were to be provided at market rates.

Also, part of the restructuring was a reduction in salaries and a re-engineering of supply management. After difficult negotiations with its Aeropers Airline Pilots Association and the Kapers cabin crew union, Swissair was able to renegotiate satisfactory employment contracts. "The strategies and measures initiated form the basis for an increase in the performance of SAirGroup," the airline stated in its annual report, "the aim is to achieve significantly improved annual results, which will ensure an appropriate return on equity as well as a profit share of our staff."

An element of Swissair's growth strategy was the decision on 4 April to create a morning peak, the fourth wave, and the concentration of all long-haul services in Zurich, much to

Lives lost

On 2 September 1998, the Swissair MD-11, HB-IWF Vaud, operated a codeshare flight 111 with Delta Air Lines from New York's JFK International to Geneva/Cointrin. The pilot-in-command was Urs Zimmermann, assisted by first officer Stefan Löw. In the cabin were the purser, 11 flight attendants and 215 passengers. Fifty-three minutes after take-off, the flight crew detected an abnormal odour in the cockpit, which they believed to have emanated from smoke in the air-conditioning system. Four minutes later, the smoke became visible, prompting the pilots to make a radio call to Moncton air traffic control, informing them of smoke in the cockpit. The crew requested a diversion to Boston Logan International, some 433 km away, but accepted Moncton ATC's offer for Halifax Stanfield International, Nova Scotia, only 122 km away. When only 56 km from the airport, the crew requested more flight distance to allow the aircraft to descend safely from its altitude 6.400 m, and also requested to dump fuel to reduce the aircraft's weight for landing. Halifax ATC vectored the aircraft towards St Margaret's Bay, where it was safe to dump fuel while remaining close to the airport. Having shut off power to the cabin, in accordance with Swissair's checklist, the fire spread to the cockpit, eventually cutting power to the autopilot. The crew informed Halifax that "we now must fly manually", before declaring an emergency. The aircraft struck the ocean some 8 km from the shore, between the tiny fishing and tourist communities of Peggy's Cove and Bayswater at an estimated speed of 565 km/h, causing it to disintegrate instantly.

The search and rescue response, crash recovery operation, and investigation by the Government of Canada took more than four years. The cockpit voice recorder (CVR) and flight data recorder (FDR) were found by the submarine HMCS Okanagan using sonar to detect the underwater locator beacon signals and were quickly retrieved by Canadian Navy divers on 11 September. Both had stopped recording when the aircraft lost electrical power at approximately 3,000 m, 5 minutes and 37 seconds before impact. The investigation carried out by the Transportation Safety Board of Canada (TSB) identified various causes and contributing factors of the crash, of which the most prominent was: Aircraft certification standards for material flammability were inadequate in that they allowed the use of materials that could be ignited and sustain or propagate fire. Consequently, flammable material propagated a fire that started above the ceiling on the right side of the cockpit near the cockpit rear wall. The fire, caused by arcing in the electrical system, spread and intensified rapidly to the extent that it degraded aircraft systems and the cockpit environment, and ultimately led to the loss of control of the aircraft. The flight was popular with United National officials, diplomates, researchers and scientists and was known as the UN Shuttle. The plane also routinely carried valuables to and from the financial capitals of the United States and Switzerland, and this flight was no different. In the cargo hold that night were millions of dollars of banknotes, jewellery and diamonds, as well as a painting La Pientre by Pablo Picasso. Two memorials to Flight 111 were erected by the Government of Nova Scotia. One at Whalesback, near Peggy's Cove, the other to the west of the crash site at Bayswater Beach Provincial Park on the Aspotogan Peninsula.

the chagrin of Geneva. To compensate, Swissair established a frequent shuttle service between Geneva and Zurich. Other significant events in 1996 included the delivery of the first 130-seat A319-100, HB-IPV *Rümlang* on 25 April, the inauguration of evening flights to New York/Newark on 1 March, and the opening of a joint Swissair/Sabena service Geneva/Zurich-Brussels on 31 March. The reason for the introduction of flights with Transwede Airways to Luleå, Sundsvall and Umeå in Sweden on 4 January, was somewhat obscure. The Fokker 100 made its last flight on 17 September, the regional type having completed 135,000 flights since 1988 without accidents. The development of the long-haul fleet was confirmed on 18 December 1996 with an order for nine Airbus A330-200 wide-body twins, powered by the Pratt & Whitney PW4168A turbofan engine, to replace the A310. A small stake was acquired in Ukraine International Airlines (UIA).

The new structure of the SAirGroup was officially established on 22 May 1997, and the re-orientation was already bearing fruit, with the airline firmly back in the black, recording a net profit of CHF 324 million. This positive development was achieved through targeted measures to improve the result against the background of an economically favourable environment, increases in productivity, consistent use of savings potentials especially in the procurement of goods and equipment, the concentration of international traffic at the Zurich hub, the optimisation of the flight schedule, fleet harmonisation, as well as the launch of attractive sales promotions. The weakening of the Swiss franc in the first half of the year also had a positive effect on the financial result. New services were introduced to Sarajevo, Ho Chi Minh City and Kuala Lumpur, the latter in a code-share with Malaysia Airlines from 1 November 1997.

The year 1998 was equally successful, but was overshadowed by the crash in Canada of the MD-11 HB-IWF *Vaud* on 2 September 1998, killing all 229 persons on board. It was the worst accident in Swissair's history. New destinations were San Francisco, Malabo, Baku, Yerevan, Tbilisi, Riga and Skopje, as well as Venice and Bologna, with aircraft painted in a special livery and the name Swissair Express, flown by Debonair. The Swissair Express services were flown by Flightline after the demise of Debonair on 1 October 1999 due to financial problems. In the long-range charter domain, Balair/CTA Leisure, LTU, Air Europe, Volare, and Sabena subsidiary Sobelair, were consolidated in the European Leisure Group.

With the delivery of the 34th aircraft of the A320 family, the renewal of the European fleet was completed, which, at the same time, ended the DC-9/MD-81 era after three decades in service with Swissair. The last flight, a special roundtrip, was completed on 3 November by HB-IND *Bachenbülach*. Four MD-11 trijets were acquired from German associate LTU, to enable the early retirement of the Boeing 747 fleet. The A330-200 orderbook was increased by four more to total 13 on 15 April 1997, followed by the signing for nine four-engined Airbus A340-600 on 19 December, for delivery in 2002/2003 as a replacement for the MD-11, although these were never delivered. The first A330-200, HB-IQA *Valais*, was delivered on 4 September 1998 and entered service in October, Swissair becoming the first European operator of the new variant. The A330-200 is a shortened version of the earlier A330-300, and provides a range of 13,400 km in a three-class configuration as applied by Swissair, which had seating for 262 passengers (22 in business, 32 in premium economy, and 208 in economy). On 12 March 1999, Swissair signed for another three aircraft, converting three earlier options, which brought the A330 fleet to 16 units.

Hunter strategy

The acquisition of a large holding in Sabena had been the forerunner of what later became known as the *Hunter Strategy*, an ambitious, high-risk (and ultimately doomed) equity-based alliance programme devised by the consulting firm of Kinsey & Company in late 1997 and implemented

Twin-engine Airbus A330-200 HB-IQG flying over the Mont Blanc massif

Sabena and Swissair aircraft at Brussels/National

by the new chief executive of the SAirGroup, Philippe Bruggisser. The reasoning behind this strategy was not difficult to work out. Swissair suffered from the classic problem of mid-sized European airlines. It was not big enough to mix it with Europe's bigger players, and not small enough to fulfil the role of a niche player, which, in any case, was considered unthinkable. It had the additional handicap to be outside the European Union and had limited access to the market. The principal aim of the *Hunter Strategy*, therefore, was to take stakes of between 10 and 25 per cent in smaller European airlines, with the objective of creating an overall 20 per cent market share. A secondary ambition was to extend this alliance building also to the long-haul market.

Over the next two years, the airline spent USD 4.2 million on taking significant shares in a number of airlines

Sabena aircraft displaying its partnership with Swissair

SAirLines Airline Equity Holdings 2000

Air Littoral (France)	49.00%
AOM (inc Air Liberté) (France)	49.50%
Austrian Airlines (Austria)	10.00%
BalairCTA Leisure (Switzerland)	100.00%
Cargolux (Luxembourg)*	33.70%
Crossair (Switzerland)	70.52%
Delta Air Lines (USA)	4.60%
LTU (Germany)	49.90%
LOT Polish Airlines (Poland)	37.60%
Luganair (Switzerland)	100.00%
PGA Portugália (Portugal)	42.00%
Sabena (Belgium)	49.50%
Singapore Airlines (Singapore)	0.62%
South African Airways (South Africa)	20.00%
Swissair Asia (Switzerland)	100.00%
TAP Air Portugal (Portugal)	34.00%
Ukraine International Airlines (Ukraine)	5.60%
Volare Group (inc Air Europe) (Italy)	49.79%

* acquired by SAirLogistics

 SOUTH AFRICAN AIRWAYS

(see table). The fact that these were largely already in financial difficulties and operated in lower market segments, eventually contributed to the unravelling of the strategy. The French airline AOM operated out of Paris/Orly and served principally destinations within France and to it Overseas Territories, while regional airline Air Littoral operated out of hubs at Nice and Montpellier to points in Southern France and to neighbouring countries. The German LTU Group connected eleven German cities to holiday destinations in Europe and further afield. At the time of the buy-in, LTU was in the midst of a major restructuring programme. Italy's Air Europe also served the holiday market, mainly in the Caribbean, but also operated scheduled services from its base of Milan/Malpensa to a number of Italian cities. Another Italian airline, Volare, had a similar *modus operandi,* combining holiday charter flights with scheduled services out of Verona and Bergamo. Private regional airline Portugália served eight European countries out of Lisbon and Porto, with the emphasis on Portugal and Spain. The Portuguese market was strengthened with the acquisition of a stake in flag-carrier TAP Air Portugal. More substantial alliances were forged with LOT Polish Airlines, which served 52 cities in 32 countries from its hub of Warsaw/Chopin, and South African Airways (SAA), which promoted route sharing between Switzerland and South Africa on a revenue-sharing basis. LOT and SAA were the only airlines to achieve a positive, albeit minimal result in 2000.

There was a flurry of activity at Swissair in 1999. On 22 June, Swissair and Sabena announced a new transatlantic co-operation with American Airlines, in response to Delta Air Lines forming a close partnership with Air France on the same day, which led to the establishment of the *SkyTeam* alliance. It was also decided to disband the *Atlantic Excellence* alliance between Swissair, Sabena, Delta and Austrian, with effect from 5 August 2000. A ten-year deal was forged with American, for which anti-trust immunity was obtained in May 2000. All services between Switzerland/Belgium and Boston, Chicago, Miami and Washington DC were switched to codeshare flights from 21 November 2000.

Another important new step was taken at the beginning of the year when the boards of Swissair and Sabena gave the green light for *Project Diamond*, to create a new airline management company, designed for closer integration between the Belgian and Swiss airlines. This led to an agreement on 26 April 2000, eventually referred to as the Airline Management Partnership (AMP), whose main provisions included an agreement for Swissair to increase its stake to 85 per cent, and granting the Belgian State 3.3 per cent share in the capital of the Swiss parent company SAirGroup. In addition, the remaining 15 per cent Sabena shares held by the Belgian State could be exchanged at a later date for an additional stake of 2.2 per cent in the SAirGroup.

Sabena would keep its status as national carrier of Belgium, with a minimum number of flights and destinations from Brussels. But a serious worsening of Sabena's financial results led to the *Blue Sky* recovery plan, which provided for a reduction in costs of EUR 357 million, including EUR 54 million resulting from a reduction in personnel costs. In addition, it included the sale of a certain number of activities to Swissair, and the closure of several routes.

However, all was not well at the Swiss group, as its financial problems threatened to overwhelm it, and its increasingly fragile relationship with Sabena. New agreements between the Belgian State and the SAirGroup were signed in January 2001, which made provisions for an increase of Sabena's resources of EUR 100 million by the State and EUR 150 million by the SAirGroup, if the *Blue Sky* recovery plan was accepted by the workforce; an undertaking by the Swiss group to take on at least 85 per cent of the catering, ground handling and cargo divisions of Sabena for EUR100-150 million; and for the SAirGroup to cover Sabena's additional cash requirements of EUR150-300 million. No sooner had the agreement been signed that, given its own financial situation, the SAirGroup threw doubt on its ability to guarantee Sabena's future. Although, after the Sabena workforce had accepted the recovery plan *in extremis*, the partners signed off on the EUR 250 million first part of the January agreement, by April 2001, the Swiss group announced that it was unwilling to inject further capital resources into Sabena, and wished to return to its original minority holding in Sabena, feeling no longer bound by the commitment to became a majority shareholder.

Flight operations underwent many changes. Several destinations were removed from the schedule for political and/or economic reasons, but new services were opened to Benghazi, its second destination in Libya, Miami and Washington DC in the United States, and Mauritius, the last-named flown by Balair with the Boeing 767. The last flight of the Airbus A310-200, HB-IPN, from New York/Newark to Basle and Zurich, ended sixteen years of service without a major accident. The last Boeing 747-300 left the fleet in January 2000. The new first-class long-haul product took to the skies for the first time on MD-11 HB-IWN. Gaby Musy-Lüthi became the first female captain at Swissair, and the airline later operated the first flight with an all-female cockpit crew.

No way back

For decades, Swissair was one of the most prestigious airlines in the world and was synonymous with Swiss quality, being known for punctuality, reliability, and excellent in-flight service. Due to its financial probity and stability, it was called the *flying bank*. But this gloss started to lose its shine in 2000, which turned out to be the worst in the airline's history. Blame for the massive net loss of CHF 2,885 million was laid at the door of overcapacity in the airline industry, high fuel costs, an unfavourable currency situation, and continued exclusion from the European market. While all these undoubtedly contributed to the poor result, there were more fundamental shortcomings that threatened its very existence. Expected, and unrealistic benefits from its airline investments failed to materialise, as management ignored the economics driving profitability, preventing it from unlocking expected synergies. Essential consolidation of routes, and rationalisation of fleets were not implemented, nor were savings achieved from purchasing services and equipment. Passenger numbers remained well below expectations.

In an effort to start afresh, without the ballast of old liabilities, the Board replaced Bruggisser by Dr Mario A Conti as President on 15 March 2001. As stated in the annual report: "The Swissair Group will undergo a strategic re-orientation, and there must be no taboos. We want to hold on to the tried and tested, but at the same time, we will adapt rapidly and vigorously to market requirements. To this end belongs an uncompromising focus on the needs of the customer and a radical simplification of existing structures". Conti devised a plan that called for the sale of aircraft and other assets, to raise an estimated CHF 4.5 billion, which would go towards paying off some of the SAirGroup's debts, that had spiralled to around CHF 15 billion by 28 September. But, given that the airline had just CHF 555 million in equity, these measures, and a proposed reduction of 1,300 personnel, were never going to be sufficient.

Then came the devastating terrorist attacks on the World Trade Centre in New York and elsewhere in the United States on 11 September and the consequent collapse of the world's air traffic. Aircraft asset values also plummeted and there were no longer realistic prospects for the sale of profitable non-flying subsidiaries to raise vital cash. With Swissair fast running out of cash, a new more radical plan was proposed on 24 September, which assumed that with Switzerland being outside the EU and would not be bound by state aid regulations, the Federal Government would bail out the airline with a rights issue. However, much to airline's surprise, the government declined and asked the Swiss banks – UBS and Credit Suisse – to prepare a rescue plan. The two banks set up a fund of CHF 1 billion (51 per cent UBS and 49 per cent CSFB), which acquired a 70 per cent stake in Crossair, and the banks were also underwriting the CHF 350 million rights issue for the remaining 30 per cent. It was also expected that the federal government and cantons would participate in this issue. The new SAir/Crossair group was to be named Swiss Air Line. Crossair was the most profitable part of the group, with salaries for cockpit and cabin crew considerably less than in the mainline operation. To further reduce costs, about 7,000 employees, some 10 per cent of the bloated staff levels, were to be dismissed.

The CEOs of the Atlantic Excellence alliance, from left: Philippe Brugisser (Swissair), Paul Reutlinger (Sabena), Mario Rehulka (Austrian) and Leo Mullin (Delta)

In the meantime, Swissair was teetering on bankruptcy and, on 29 September, the banks agreed to purchase a share in Crossair for CHF 260 million, and provide Swissair with an interim credit of CHF 250 million to guarantee flights until 3 October. However, due to disagreements between the government, the airline and the banks, the signing of the contracts and transfer of funds was delayed and all flights were halted on 2 October 2001, leaving 19,000 passengers and crew stranded worldwide and their tickets were not accepted by other airlines. They were offered neither alternative flights nor cash to get home. Swissair did not have the funds to pay for fuel and airport taxes and had to declare bankruptcy. The international press called Swissair's collapse a "national tragedy", having caused untold damage to Switzerland's standing in the world, with some going even further, calling it a Swiss humiliation. It was a failure on a previously unknown scale in the Swiss business world. Unsurprisingly, there was an immediate outcry from politicians, the Swissair management and the public, with the blame for the fiasco laid firmly at the door of UBS, which, in one newspaper was renamed UBS-United Bandits of Switzerland. Unexpectedly, on 3 October, the *Bundesrat* (upper house of parliament), presenting itself belatedly as the saviour of the nation, agreed a federal credit of CHF 450 million, which enabled Swissair to continue operating flights from 5 October, albeit at a much-reduced level, and its European network handed over to Crossair. It is ironic that having failed to save its national carrier, it was quick to rescue a tottering UBS from bankruptcy in autumn 2008.

Swissair's collapse also had a knock-on effect elsewhere. A Swiss compromise for yet another restructuring plan by Sabena in the summer of 2001 had been rejected by the Belgian State, which instigated legal proceedings against Swissair on 3 July, joined by Sabena on 10 July. In a final attempt to resolve the impasse and reach a solution that would be acceptable to both parties, an agreement was signed on 2 August, of which the main provisions were as follows: The SAirGroup was released from its obligation to become the majority shareholder, in exchange for making a final financial injection of EUR 258 million, to which the Belgian State would add another EUR 172 million, for a total of EUR 430 million. This was to be made in four instalments over a two-year period. The SAirGroup also agreed to take over nine Airbus A319s ordered by Sabena and, furthermore, the Belgian State and Sabena would halt their legal proceedings.

On 1 October, Swissair informed Sabena and the Belgian government that it would not be able to honour its promised financial commitment and it quickly became clear that the days of the Belgian national airline were numbered. The European Commission authorised a rescue aid loan of EUR 125 million by the Belgian authorities, limited in time, and linked to a fundamental restructuring plan. But it was far too late to save Sabena. Accepting that no recovery plan had a chance of succeeding and that there was no candidate willing to take over the airline, abandoned by the Belgian State, Sabena was declared bankrupt on 7 November 2001.

Swissair continued reduced operations during the winter months, guaranteed through a CHF 1,1 billion credit line from the government, until the last flight from São Paulo landed at Zurich on 1 April 2002. On that same day, now owned by UBS, Credit Suisse, the Swiss Confederation and cantons and communities, Crossair started operations as SWISS International Air Lines, SWISS for short, taking over Swissair's intercontinental routes, and most aircraft and assets. It signified the final end of Swissair. SWISS struggled in the early years and did not record its first net profit until 2006. A decision had already been made to align itself with another airline, rather than remain a niche carrier, and, on 1 July 2007, it was taken over by Lufthansa, but continues serving as Switzerland's flag-carrier under the SWISS name.

Swissair Fleet 1931-2002

BFW/Messerschmitt M 18 d 1931-1937 (1)

Four-passenger cantilever shoulder-wing monoplane, powered by a 171 KW (230 hp) Armstrong Siddeley Lynx engine, generating a cruising speed of 140 km/h

CH-191	476	26.03.31-01.10.24	reregistered HB-IME
HB-IME	476	01.10.34-25.01.38	ex CH-191; to Farnerwerke, Grenchen, Switzerland as HB-IME

Comte AC-4 Gentleman (1931-1948) (1)

Two-passenger strut-braced high-wing monoplane, powered by a 78 kW (105 hp) Cirrus Hermes III engine, generating a cruising speed of 140 km/h

CH-262	34	26.03.31-01.10.34	reregistered HB-IKO
HB-IKO	34	01.10.34-00.11.47	ex CH-262; to A Kammacher as

Dornier Do B Bal Merkur 1931-1932 (2)

Eight-passenger strut-braced high-wing monoplane, powered by a 373 kW (500 hp) BMW Viu engine, generating a cruising speed of 180 km/h

CH-142		26.03.31-08.10.32	never used and broken up
CH-171		26.03.31-08.10.32	never used and broken up

Fokker F.VIIa 1931-1950 (1)

Eight passenger high-wing cantilever monoplane, powered a 123 kW (165 hp) Gnome-Rhône Jupiter IV engine, generating a cruising speed of 185 km/h

CH-157	5005	26.03.31-01.10.34	reregistered HB-LBO
HB-LBO	5005	01.10.34-00.00.50	ex CH-157; preserved at the Verkehrshaus, Lucerne, Switzerland since 1972

Fokker F.VIIb-3m 1931-1935 (8)

10-passenger high-wing canitlever monoplane, powered by three 150 kW (200 hp) Armstrong Siddeley Lynx Mk.IV engines, generating a cruising speed of 190 km/h

CH-162	5208	26.03.31-25.05.35	allotted HB-LBQ but ntu; to Ala Littoria as I-AFRO
CH-163	5209	26.03.31-08.06.35	allotted HB-LBR but ntu; to Ala Littoria as I-UGRI
CH-164	5210	26.03.31-31.05.35	allotted HB-LBS but ntu; to Ala Littoria as I-UADI
CH-165	5105	26.03.31-01.10.34	ex H-NADR; reregistered HB-LAN
CH-166	5238	26.03.31-01.10.34	reregistered HB-LAO
CH-190	5128	26.03.31-12.04.35	allotted HB-LAK but ntu; cannibalised for repairs to CH-166 after crash-landing at Promsens, Switzerland

CH-192	5225	26.03.31-02.02.34	to Emperor Haile Selassie I, Ethiopia
CH-193	5136	26.03.31-19.06.31	destroyed by fire during refuelling at Paris/Le Bourget
HB-LAN	5105	01.10.34-23.06.35.35	ex CH-165; to Ala Littoria as I-UEBI
HB-LAO	5238	01.10.34-1.10.35	ex CH-166; to Ala Littoria as I-ADUA

Lockheed 9B Orion 1932-1936 (2)

Four-passenger low-wing cantilever monoplane, powered by a 429 kW (575 hp) Wright 1820-E Cyclone engine, generating a cruising speed of 290 km/h

CH-167	189	07.04.32-01.10.34	ex NC12231; reregistered HB-LAH
CH-168	190	07.04.32-01.10.34	ex NC12232; reregistered HB-LAJ
HB-LAH	189	01.10.34-28.10.36	ex CH-167; to Spanish Republican Air force but never collected and dismantled
HB-LAJ	190	01.10.34-28.10.36	ex CH-168; to Spanish Republican Air Force but never collected and dismantled

Clark GA 43 1934-1936 (2)

10-passenger low-wing all-metal monoplane, powered by a 537 kW (720 hp) Wright SR-1820-F2 Cyclone engine, generaqting a cruising speed of 240 km/h

CH-169	2202	16.03.34-01.10.34	reregistered HB-LAM
HB-LAM	2202	01.10.34-28.10.36	ex CH-169; to Spanish Republican Air Force
HB-ITU	2204	19.03.35-30.04.36	crashed into Rigi Mountain, Switzerland through disorientation in fog at night

Curtiss AT-32 C 1934 (1)

15-passenger composite construction biplane, powered by two 537 kW (720 hp) Wright SR-1820-F2 Cyclone engine, generating a cruising speed of 245 km/h

| CH-170 | 53 | 11.04.34-27.07.34 | allotted HB-LAP but ntu; crashed near Tuttlingen, Germany on approach to Stuttgart/Echterdingen |

Douglas DC-2 1934-1952 (6)

14-passenger low-wing all-metal cantilever monoplane, powered by two 537 kW (720 hp) Wright SGR-1820-F2a engines, generating a cruising speed of 240 km/h

HB-ISA	1320	07.04.36-28.10.36	ex A-500; to Spanish Republican Air Force
HB-ISI	1331	22.7.35-09.08.44	destroyed on ground at Stuttgart/Echterdingen by US air attack
HB-ITA	1329	29.01.35-07.01.39	crashed near Senlis on approach to Paris/Le Bourget
HB-ITE	1322	17.01.35-18.03.52	to Phoenix Airlines as ZS-DFW
HB-ITI	1321	04.12.34-28.02.36	crashed on take-off from Zurich/Dübendorf
HB-ITO	1332	15.02.35-18.03.52	to Phoenix Airlines as ZS-DFX

Junker Ju 86 1936-1939 (2)

10-passenger low-wing all-metal cantilever monoplane, powered by two 447 kW (600 hp) Junkers Jumo 205C diesel engines, generating a cruising speed of 285 km/h

HB-IXA	0860951	00.02.39-20.07.39	ex HB-IXE; damaged beyond repair in crash-landing near Constance
HB-IXE	0860951	16.03.37-00.02.39	reregistered HB-IXA
HB-IXI	086008'	01.04.36-12.08.36	crash-landed near Wixhausen, Germany and returned to Junkers

de Havilland D.H.89 Dragon Six 1937-1954 (1)

Eight-passenger light transport biplane, powered by two 150 kW (200 hp) de Havilland Gipsy Six piston engines, generating a maximum speed of 250 km/h

HB-ARA	6250		reregistered HB-APA
HB-APA	6250	20.03.37-24.06.54	ex HB-ARA; to Farnerwerke, Grenchen, Switzerland

Douglas DC-3/C-47 1937-1969 (16)

21-passengers low-wing, all-metal monoplane, powered by two 895 kW (1,200 hp) Pratt & Whitney R-1830-S1C3G Twin Wasp engines, generating a speed of 370 km/h

HB-IRA	DC-3	1945	10.06.37-30.03.55	to Fleetwings Inc as N2815D
HB-IRB	DC-3D	42969	20.03.46-19.06.62	to Riis Flyrederei as LN-LMK
HB-IRC	DC-3D	42978	18.04.46-09.05.69	to Protea Airways as ZS-FRJ
HB-IRD	C-47B-5-DK	14609/26054	15.02.46-26.04.50	ex USAAF 43-48793; to Israel Defense Forces (IDF) as 1408/4X-ACW
HB-IRE	DC-3	2121	10.05.39-18.02.55	to Fleetwings Inc as N2818D
HB-IRF	C-47B-10-DK	15020/26465	29.05.46-18.11.60	ex USAAF 43-49204; to Spantax as EC-AQF
HB-IRG	C-47B1-DK	14196/25641	04.02.46-08.10.60	ex USAAF 43-48380; to Spantax as EC-AQE
HB-IRH	C-47A-25-DK	13483	24.08.51-26.09.52	ex ET-T-15; leased from Ethiopian Airlines
HB-IRI	DC-3	1946	22.06.37-28.03.55	to Fleetwings Inc as N2816D
HB-IRK	C-47B-1-DL	20737	10.09.47-18.06.57	ex USAAF 43-16281; crashed into Lake Constance while on training flight
HB-IRL	C-47B-10-DK	14814/26259	30.01.47-05.02.61	ex RAF KJ966; to Katanga as KA-DFN
HB-IRM	C-47B-30-DK	16191/32939	10.04.47-23.02.61	ex RAF KN465; to Moroccan Air Force as CN-ALB
HB-IRN	C-47B-35-DK	16645/33393	08.03.47-13.05.69	ex RAF KN683; to Verkehrshaus, Lucerne, Switzerland for display
HB-IRO	DC-3	2054	31.10.38-08.03.55	to Fleetwings Inc as N2817D
HB-IRU	DC-3	2132	08.08.39-25.05.40	to AB Aerotransport as SE-BAG
HB-IRX	C-47B-5-DK	14717/26162	11.07.47-06.06.69	ex HB-ATI; used as a freighter; to Ethiopian Airlines as ET-ADC

de Havilland D.H.98 Mosquito PR Mk.IV 1945 (1)

Shoulder-wing photo-reconnaissance aircraft, powered by two 932 kW (1,250 hp) Rolls-Royce Merlin engines, generating a cruising speed of 620 km/h

HB-IMO		00.00.45-07.08.45	ex RAF DK310; leased from SWISS Air Force for airmail tests

Douglas DC-4-1009 1946-1959 (5)

40-passenger low-wing, all-metal monoplane powered by four 1,082 kW (1,450 hp) Pratt & Whitney R-2000-2SD13-G Twin Wasp engines, generating a maximum speed of 450 km/h

HB-ILA	*Uri*	43072	24.11.46-29.05.59	to Balair as HB-ILA
HB-ILE		43093	15.02.47-13.12.50	crashed on approach to Sydney, Nova Scotia, Canada
HB-ILI	*Basel/Schwyz*	43097	26.04.47-20.10.58	to Syrian Airways as YK-AAR
HB-ILO		43098	30.04.47-14.12.51	crashed on approach to Amsterdam/Schiphol, Netherlands
HB-ILU*	*Unterwalden/ Nidwalden*	27289	02.04.52-10.04.59	ex N88887; to Balair as HB-ILU

* Douglas C-54E-5-DO

Nord 1000 1946-1953 (1)

Three-passenger low-wing cantilever monoplane, powered by a 179 kW (240 hp) Renault 6Q-10 engine, generating a speed of 260 km/h

HB-IKI	35	20.12.46-29.05.53	ex HB-OAZ; to Eidgenössisches Luftamt

Mraz K-65 Cap 1948-1950 (1)

High-wing strut-braced liaison monoplane, powered by a 179 kW (240 hp) Argus As 10C engine, generating a speed of 175 km/h

HB-IKA	741	22.01.48-05.10.50	to Lindt & Sprüngli, Kilchberg, Switzerland

de Havilland D.H.89A Dragon Rapide 1948-1954 (2)

Eight-passenger light transport biplane, powered by two 150 kW (200 hp) de Havilland Gipsy Six piston engines, generating a maximum speed of 250 km/h

HB-APE	6437	19.04.48-24.06.54	ex HB-AME; to Farnerwerke, Grenchen, Switzerland
HB-APU	6438	14.05.48-24.06.54	ex HB-AMU; to Farnerwerke, Grenchen, Switzerland

Convair 240 1949-1957 (8)

40-passenger short-range airliner, powered by two 1,800 kW (2,400 hp) Pratt & Whitney R-2800-CA3 Double Wasp radial engines, generating a cruising speed of 465 km/h

HB-IMA	Ticino	144	07.07.54-29.08.56	ex PH-TEL; to Mohawk Airlines as N1020C
HB-IRP	Graubünden	113	11.02.49-10.01.57	to Mohawk Airlines as N1013C
HB-IRS	Glarus	132	18.02.49-10.05.57	to Mohawk Airlines as N1017C
HB-IRT	Appenzell	133	17.02.49-18.10.56	to Mohawk Airlines as N1018C
HB-IRV	Neuchâtel	134	28.02.49-02.11.56	to Mohawk Airlines as N1019C
HB-IRW	Ticino	61	28.11.53-19.06.54	ex PH-TEA; crashed into English Channel off Folkstone
HB-IRY	Luzern	111	17.11.53-25.08.56	ex PH-TEE; to Mohawk Airlines as N1012C
HB-IRZ	Valais	124	12.12.53-10.10.56	ex PH-TEH; to Mohawk Airlines as N1014C

Douglas DC-6B 1951-1964 (8)

68-passenger, low-wing monoplane, powered by four 1,865 kW (2,500 hp) Pratt & Whitney R-2800-CB17 Double Wasp engines, generating a speed of 510 km/h

HB-IBA	Zürich/Aargau	43274	24.06.51-22.08.62	to Sterling Airways as OY-EAO
HB-IBB*		45551	02.10.58-16.06.61	to World Airways as N45501
HB-IBC	Nidwalden	43547	15.06.58-15.07.61	ex N90764; leased from American Airlines
HB-IBE	Genève	43275	18.07.51-16.06.62	to Sterling Airways as OY-EAN
HB-IBI	St Gallen	43750	23.10.52-16.11.62	to Sterling Airways as OY-EAP
HB-IBO	Bern/Luzern	44087	14.10.53-01.05.64	leased to Finlantic as OH-DCB 09.10.62-00.05.63; to Olympic Airways as SX-DAM
HB-IBU	Vaud	44088	26.10.53-14.03.62	to Balair as HB-IBU
HB-IBZ	Basel-Land	44089	26.10.53-14.03.61	to Balair as HB-IBZ

* Douglas DC-6A

Convair 440 Metropolitan 1956-1968 (12)

52-passenger low-wing monoplane, powered by two 1,865 kW (2,500 hp) Pratt & Whitney R-2800-CB16 Double Wasp engines, generating a speed of 465 km/h

HB-IMB	Fribourg	327	07.06.56-31.08.67	to Luftwaffe as CA+034
HB-IMC	Appenzell AR/ Luzern	332	27.06.56-01.11.66	to Martinair Holland as PH-MAL
HB-IMD		335	13.07.56-15.07.56	crashed on delivery flight on approach to Sannon, Ireland
HB-IMF	Ticino	355	02.08.56-10.02.67	crashed into Hochwacht, Switzerland on training flight
HB-IMG	Appenzell IR	360	29.08.56-22.12.68	to Great Lakes Airlines as CF-GLC
HB-IMH	Graubünden	363	19.09.56-22.09.66	to HR-SAP
HB-IMK	Neuchâtel	364	26.09.56-01.11.68	to Great Lakes Airlines as CF-GLD
HB-IML	Glarus	365	28.09.56-19.10.68	to HR-SAU
HB-IMM*	Valais	412	28.03.57-05.04.68	to SATA as HB-IMM
HB-IMN	Zug	413	04.04.57-01.11.68	to Pan Adria as YU-ADS
HB-IMP	Thurgau	414	10.04.57-01.11.68	to Pan Adria as YU-ADT
HB-IMR	Obwalden	429	28.05.57-27.10.66	to Luftwaffe as CA+035

* believed converted to Convair 640

Douglas DC-7C 1956-1962 (5)

105-passenger low-wing monoplane, powered by four 2,536 kW (3,400 hp) Pratt & Whitney R-3350EA1 engines, generating a maximum speed of 650 km/h

HB-IBK	*Zürich*	45061	08.11.56-28.02.62	to Scandinavian Airlines System (SAS) as LN-MOG
HB-IBL	*Genève*	45062	06.12.56-20.07.60	to Riddle Airlines as N301G
HB-IBM	*Basel Stadt*	45190	01.06.57-02.04.62	to Riddle Airlines as N302G
HB-IBN	*Bern*	45191	07.08.57-30.11.60	to Riddle Airlines as N8218H
HB-IBP	*Schwyz*	45553	04.11.58-05.11.61	to Scandinavian Airlines System (SAS) as SE-CCH

Scottish Aviation Twin Pioneer 1957 (1)

16-passenger high-wing STOL light transport, powered by two 403 kW (540 hp) Alvis Leonides 514/8 air-cooled radian engines, generating a cruising speed of 190 km/h

G-AOEO		503	04.01.57-04.04.57	test flying into high-altitude airports in the Alps

Douglas DC-8-30 1960-1976 (3)

177-passenger medium/long-range aircraft, powered by four 78.4kN Pratt & Whitney JT4A-11 turbojet engines, generating a speed of 895 km/h

HB-IDA	*Matterhorn/ Genève*	45416/54	20.04.60-15.03.68	to Südflug as D-ADIM
HB-IDB*	*Jungfrau/Basel Stadt*	45417/69	18.06.60-25.02.76	to SATA as HB-IDB
HB-IDC	*Piz Bernina/ Zürich*	45526/98	29.08.60-23.12.67	to Südflug as D-ADIR

* converted to Douglas DC-8-50

Sud-Aviation SE-210 Caravelle III 1960-1971 (9)

80-passenger short/medium-range aircraft, powered by two rear-mounted 50.7 kN (11,400 lb) Rolls-Royce Avon Mk.527 turbojet engines, generating a speed of 805 km/h

HB-ICR		119	28.02.64-04.03.66	ex F-BJTJ; leased from Air France
HB-ICS	*Uri*	121	17.03.62-10.04.71	to China airlines as B-1850
HB-ICT	*Schwyz*	122	29.03.62-12.01.71	to China airlines as B-1852
HB-ICU	*Aargau*	123	19.04.62-20.10.70	to Sobelair as OO-SBQ
HB-ICV	*Schaffhausen*	147	19.10.62-04.09.63	crashed near Dürrenasch, Switzerland
HB-ICW	*Solothurn*	33	30.04.60-00.01.69	lease/purchased from SAS; to Transavia as PH-TRO
HB-ICX	*Chur*	38	24.06.60-23.03.71	lease/purchased from SAS; to Catair as F-BSRD
HB-ICY	*Lausanne*	43	08.07.60-11.11.69	lease/purchased from SAS; to Transavia as PH-TRP
HB-ICZ	*Bellinzona*	48	13.08.60-25.03.70	lease/purchased from SAS; leased to Air Algerie in 1969; to Transavia as PH-TRR

Convair 880-22M 1961-1962 (2)

110-passenger narrow-body aircraft, powered by four 51.8 kN (11,650 lb) General Electric CJ-805-3B turbofan engines, generating a cruising speed of 990 km/h

HB-ICL		22-00-45M	11.08.61-19.05.62	ex N8485H; leased from Convair
HB-ICM		22-00-43M	20.06.61-19.05.62	ex N8487H; leased from Convair

Convair 990-30A Coronado 1962-1975 (8)

130-passenger narrowbody aircraft, powered by four 71.4 kN (16,050 lb) General Electric CJ805-23B turbofan engines, generating a speed of 1,000 km/h

HB-ICA	*Bern*	30-10-7	12.01.62-17.04.75	to Spantax as EC-CNG
HB-ICB	*Luzern*	30-10-11	17.01.62-29.04.75	to MBB and broken up at Hamburg/Finkenwerder
HB-ICC	*St Gallen*	30-10-12	25.01.62-30.03.75	displayed at Verkehrshaus, Lucerne
HB-ICD	*Basel-Land*	30-10-15	03.02.62-21.02.70	crashed near Würenlingen, Switzerland
HB-ICE	*Vaud*	30-10-14	03.08.62-07.06.75	to Spantax as EC-CNJ
HB-ICF	*Schaffhausen*	30-10-6	01.02.64-26.04.75	to MBB and broken up at Hamburg/Finkenwerder
HB-ICG	*Winterthur,* later			
	Grisons/ Graubünden	30-10-8	17.02.62-05.04.75	leased to SAS as SE-DAY until 22.02.66; to Spantax as EC-CNF
Hb-ICH	*St Gotthard*	30-10-17	10.04.62-31.05.75	leased to SAS as SE-DAZ until 22.02.66; leased to Balair 26.03.68-30.03.71; to Spantax as EC-CNH

Douglas DC-8-50 1963-1970 (2)

189-passenger long-range aircraft, powered by four 80.6 kN (18,200 lb) Pratt & Whitney JT3D-3B turbofan engines, generating a speed of 865 km/h

HB-IDB*	*Basel Stadt*	45417/69	18.06.60-25.02.76	to SATA as HB-IDB
HB-IDD	*Nidwalden*	45656/191	26.10.63-13.09.70	hi-jacked and blown up at Zerqa (Dawson'a Field), Jordan

* converted from Douglas DC-8-30

Line-up of Caravelle HB-ICW and three Convair 990

Fokker F.27-400 Friendship 1965-1972 (3)

56-seat short/medium-range high-wing aircraft, powered by two 1,678 kW (2,250 hp) Rolls-Royce Dart Mk.532-7 turboprop engines, generating a speed of 460km/h

HB-AAV	10276	11.06.65-07.03.72	operated by Balair; to NLM Cityhopper as PH-FKD
HB-AAW*	10323	23.03.67-16.09.71	operated by Balair; to Gulf Aviation as G-AZFD
HB-AAX	10351	30.01.68-07.02.72	operated by Balair; to NLM Cityhopper as PH-KFE

* Fokker F.27-600

Douglas DC-9-15 1966-1968 (5)

90-passenger short-range aircraft, powered by two rear-mounted 62.2 kN (14,000 lb) Pratt & Whitney JT8D-7 turbofan engines, generating a speed of 895 km/h

HB-IFA	*Graubünden*	45731/34	15.07.66-18.09.68	returned to McDonnell Douglas as N8500
HB-IFB	*Obwalden*	45732/41	01.08.66-14.06.68	returned to McDonnell Douglas and sold to FAA as N119
HB-IFC	*Appenzell Ausserrhoden*	45785/64	30.11.66-21.08.68	returned to McDonnell Douglas as N1790U
HB-IFD	*Glarus*	45786/90	10.03.67-31.08.68	returned to McDonnell Douglas as N1791U
HB-IFE	*Ticino*	45787/127	26.06.67-09.09.68	returned to McDonnell Douglas as N1793U

McDonnell Douglas DC-8-62 1967-1984 (7)

189-passenger long-range aircraft, powered by four 80.6 kN (18,200 lb) Pratt & Whitney JT3D-3B turbofan engines, generating a speed of 865 km/h

HB-IDE	*Genève/Uri*	45919/312	23.11.67-08.10.79	crashed on landing at Athens, Greece
HB-IDF	*Zürich/Schwyz*	45920/319	02.01.67-09.10.83	to Capitol Air as N923CL
HB-IDG	*Matterhorn/ Neuchâtel*	45925/333	24.02.68-15.09.83	to Capitol Air as N922CL
HB-IDH*	*Piz Bernina*	45984/370	11.07.68-01.04.76	to Balair as HB-IDH
HB-IDI	*Solothurn*	46077/470	05.07.69-11.04.84	to United Air Carriers as N923R
HB-IDK*	*Matterhorn*	46078/475	06.08.69-26.12.81	to Peruvian Air Force as FAP370/OB-1372
HB-IDL	*Aargau*	45417/69	06.02.70-26.04.84	to Capitol Air as N924CL

* McDonnell Douglas DC-8-62CF

McDonnell Douglas DC-9-32 1967-1988 (22)

115-passenger short/medium-range aircraft, powered by two rear-mounted 64.5 kN (14,500 lb) Pratt & Whitney JT9D-9 turbofan engined, generating a speed of 895 km/h engines, generating a speed of 895 km/h

HB-IDO	*Cointrin*	47480/607	08.10.70-18.12.87	to Northwest Airlines as N986US
HB-IDP	*Basel-Land*	47523/523	18.11.70-29.09.88	to British Midland Aireats as G-PKBE

HB-IDR	Baden	47535/610	03.12.70-30.09.81	to Texas International Airlines as N542TX
HB-IFF	Fribourg	45788/171	21.10.67-10.11.76	to Texas International Airlines as N3505T
HB-IFG	Valais	45789/217	23.12.67-11.08.81	to Texas International Airlines as N543TX
HB-IFH	Opfikon/Baden	45790/264	28.02.68-22.11.88	to Northwest Airlines as N982US
HB-IFI	Zug	45971/349	28.07.68-22.12.80	to Texas International Airlines as N532TX
HB-IFK	Kloten	45972/372	11.09.68-28.04.82	leased to Spantax as EC-DQP; to as N539TX
HB-IFL	Appenzell Innerrhoden	45973/381	28.09.68-20.11.81	to Texas International Airlines as N541TX
HB-IFM	Thurgau	45847/394	17.10.68-01.10.80	to Texas International Airlines as N531TX
HB-IFN	Obwalden	47094/149	29.05.68-13.07.81	leased from new to SAS as SE-DBZ; to Texas International Airlines as N545TX
HB-IFO	Appenzell Ausserrhoden	47110/167	09.08.68-26.03.81	leased from new to SAS as OY-KGU; to Texas International Airlines as N534TX
HB-IFP	Glarus	47111/182	21.08.68-00.04.81	leased from new to SAS as LN-LRS until; to Texas International Airlines as N535TX
HB-IFR	Ticino	47112/199	30.08.68-31.08.81	leased from new to SAS as SE-DBY; to Texas International Airlines as N537TX
HB-IFS	Graubünden/ Grisons	47113/213	06.09.68-19.06.81	leased from new to SAS as OY-KGW; to Texas International Airlines as N536TX
HB-IFT	Rümlang	47281/427	19.12.68-14.01.81	to Texas International Airlines as N533TX
HB-IFU	Chur	47282/446	31.01.69-01.07.88	to Northwest Airlines as N983US
HB-IFV	Bülach	47383/538	03.10.69-24.10.88	to Northwest Airlines as N984US
HB-IFW*	Payerne	47384/543	20.10.69-06.05.84	to Airborne Express as N931AX
HB-IFX	Lausanne	47218/312	20.10.68-28.12.81	ex D-ACEB; to Texas International Airlines as N538TX
HB-IFY	Bellinzona	47219/325	22.10.68-07.10.81	ex D-ACEC; to Texas International Airlines as N544TX
HB-IFZ	Dübendorf	47479/605	18.09.70-18.05.79	delivered to Balair but used by SWISSair

BAC One-Eleven 1967-1970 (3)

119-passenger short-range narrow-body aircraft, powered by two rear-mounted Rolls-Royce Spey turbofan engines, generating a speed of 880 km/h

G-ATPK	1-11-301AG	34	15.11.67-29.04.68	leased from British Eagle Airways
G-ATVH	1-11-207AJ	40	01.04.67-14.11.67	ex 9J-RCI; leased from British Eagle Airways
G-AWYS	1-11-501EX	175	23.04.70-31.10.70	leased from British United Airways (BUA)

Boeing 747-200B 1971-1984 (2)

440-passenger wide-body intercontinental airliner, powered by four 253 kN (56,900 lb) General Electric CF6-50E2 turbofan engines, generating a speed of 895 km/h

HB-IGA	Genève	20116/112	29.01.71-01.01.84	to Salenia as LX-SAL
HB-IGB	Zürich	20117/126	25.03.71-16.01.84	to National Airlines as OH-KSA

McDonnell Douglas DC-10-30 1972-1992 (14)

270-passenger long-range wide-body aircraft, powered by three 227 kN (51,000 lb) General Electric CF6-50C turbofan engines, generating a speed of 895 km/h

HB-IHA	*St Gallen*	46575/57	30.11.72-02.09.83	ex N134UO; to Ecuatoriana as HC-BKO
HB-IHB	*Schaffhausen*	46576/73	05.02.73-09.04.84	to Spantax as EC-DUG
HB-IHC	*Luzern/ Obwalden*	46577/114	10.09.73-13.09.91	to Northwest airlines as N220NW
HB-IHD	*Bern/Thurgau*	46578/131	06.12.73-01.05.88	to JAT-Yugoslav Airlines as YU-AMC
HB-IHE	*Vaud*	46579/132	06.02.74-24.05.91	to Northwest Airlines as N221NW
HB-IHF	*Nidwalden*	46580/83	11.01.75-21.10.91	to Northwest airlines as N223NW
HB-IHG	*Grisons/ Graubünden*	46581/184	14.02.75-30.05.91	to Northwest airlines as N224NW
HB-IHH	*Basel Stadt/ Schaffhausen*	46582/187	21.02.75-18.02.92	to Northwest airlines as N224NW
HB-IHI	*Fribourg*	46969/241	21.10.77-23.06.92	to Northwest airlines as N227NW
HB-IHL	*Ticino/ Thurgau*	46583/292	03.03.80-27.02.92	converted to DC-10-30ER; to Northwest Airlines as N226NW
HB-IHM	*Valais/Wallis*	46584/292	01.02.80-02.08.92	converted to DC-10-30ER; to Continental Airlines as N15069
HB-IHN*	*St Gallen*	48292/368	27.02.82-15.05.92	sold to Continental Airlines as N87070
HB-IHO*	*Uri*	48293/371	28.09.89-23.01.91	to Continental Airlines as N83071
HB-IHP		46868/171	28.09.89-23.01.91	ex LN-RKA; to Northwest Airlines as N211NW

* McDonnell Souglas DC-10-30ER

Douglas DC-9-41 1974-1975 (4)

125-passenger short/medium-range aircraft, powered by two rear-mounted 66.7 kN (15,000 lb) Pratt & Whitney JT8D-11 turbofan engines, generating a speed of 895 km/h

HB-IDV	47118/308	12.12.74-22.08.75	ex LN-RLK; leased from SAS
HB-IDW	47115/261	01.10.74-03.10.75	ex OY-KGA; leased from SAS
HB-IDX	47117/319	30.10.74-09.10.75	ex SE-DBW; leased from SAS
HB-IDY	47395/555	21.11.74-26.09.75	ex OY-KGG; leased from SAS

Douglas DC-9-51 1975-1988 (12)

139-seat short/medium-range aircraft, powered by two rear-mounted 69 kN (15,000 lb) Pratt & Whitney JT8D-15A turbofan engines, generating a speed of 895 km/h

HB-ISK	*Höri*	47654/757	19.11.75-01.10.86	to Hawaiian Airlines as N669HA
HB-ISL	*Köniz*	47665/763	12.09.75-07.04.87	to SAS as LN-RMC
HB-ISM	*Wettingen*	47656/783	14.08.75-07.06.88	to Guiness Peat Aviation (GPA) as EI-BWA
HB-ISN	*Sion*	47657/787	11.09.75-30.10.87	to SAS as SE-DFN
HB-ISO	*Biel/Bienne*	47658/790	29.09.75-19.02.88	to SAS as SE-DFO

HB-ISP	Lugano	47659/807	12.02.76-04.10.83	to Muse Air as N670MC
HB-ISR	Locarno	47660/810	22.02.76-14.10.83	to Muse Air as N671MC
HB-ISS	Dietlikon	47661/812	10.03.76-05.01.84	to Muse Air as N672MC
HB-IST	Aarau	47662/850	04.02.77-13.02.86	to Hawaiian Airlines as N679HA
HB-ISU	Bachenbülach	47663/851	16.02.77-10.04.86	to Hawaiian Airlines as N689HA
HB-ISV	Winkel	47783/899	07.03.79-17.10.88	to Linea Aeropostal Venezolana (LAV) as YV-40C
HB-ISW	Dübendorf	47784/902	02.05.79-05.08.88	to Linea Aeropostal Venezolana (LAV) as YV-41C

McDonnell Douglas MD-81 (DC-9-81)/MD-82/83 1981-1998 (27)

172-seat short/medium-range aircraft, powered by two rear-mounted 80 kN (18,000 lb) Pratt & Whitney JT8D-217A turbofan engines, generating a speed of 875 km/h

HB-INA	Höri	49100/1025	09.12.81-06.10.97	to TWA as N924TW
HB-INB		49101/1050	17.03.82-01.08.96	operated by Balair 01.04.82-01.03.95; to TWA as N921TW
HB-INC	Thurgau, Lugano	48002/938	12.09.80-29.03.96	to SAS as SE-DMX
HB-IND	Zug, Bachenbülach	48003/944	26.10.80-08.12.97	to SAS as SE-DMT
HB-INE	Rümlang	48004/950	21.11.80-01.05.96	leased to Air Afrique 82/83; to SAS as OY-KIK
HB-INF	Appenzell a. Rh.,			
	Steinmaur	48005/957	28.01.81-31.05.96	to SAS as SE-DMU
HB-ING	Glarus, Winkel	48006/966	03.04.81-24.03.95	to SAS as OY-KIG
HB-INH	Winterthur	48007/971	07.05.81-13.04.95	to SAS as OY-KIH
HB-INI	Kloten	48008/981	01.07.81-17.07.95	to SAS as OY-KII
HB-INK	Opfikon	48009/985	20.06.81-13.06.95	to SAS as SE-DMZ
HB-INL	Jura, Embach	48010/992	24.07.81-07.11.95	to SAS as SE-DMY
HB-INM	Lausanne	48011/994	05.08.81-27.02.97	to McDonnell Douglas as N532MD
HB-INN	Appenzell i. Rh., Bülach	48012/997	29.08.81-23.07.97	to TWA as N928TW
HB-INO	Bellinzona	48013/1000	05.08.81-27.02.97	to TWA as N922TW
HB-INP	Oberglatt	48014/1013	30.10.81-14.08.97	to TWA as N929TW
HB-INR		49277/1181	21.02.93-05.08.95	leased from Balair
HB-INS	Meyrin	49356/1250	25.01.86-09.10.97	to TWA as N926TW
HB-INT	Grand Saconnex	49357/1251	14.02.86-09.04.97	to TWA as N925TW
HB-INU	Vernier	49358/1254	28.07.86-12.12.97	to TWA as N927TW
HB-INV	Dübendorf	49359/1349	18.03.87-31.10.95	to Crossair as HB-INV
HB-INX	Wallisellen	49570/1440	02.05.88-13.02.98	to Spanair as EC-GTO
HB-INY	Bassersdorf	49571/1458	00.03.88-00.11.97	to Spanair as EC-GQZ
HB-INZ	Regensdorf	49572/1468	06.05.88-27.10.97	to Crossair as HB-INZ
HB-ISX	Binningen	49442/1358	31.03.89-21.04.96	to Crossair as HB-ISX

HB-IUG	*Illnau-Effretikon*	53149/1817	21.01.91-01.02.96	to Crossair as HB-IUG
HB-IUH	*Wangen-Brüttisellen*	53150/1831	08.03.91-01.03.96	to Crossair as HB-IUH
PH-MBZ		49144/1096	01.04.89-21.10.89	leased from Martinair Holland

Airbus A310-200 1983-1999 (5)

265-passenger medium-range wide-body aircraft, powered by two 257 kN (57,900 lb) General Electric CF6-80A3 turbofan engines, generating a speed of 850 km/h

HB-IPA	*Aargau*	224	25.03.83-21.04.95	to FedEx as N446FE *Makenna*
HB-IPB	*Neuchâtel*	251	30.05.83-31.07.96	to FedEx as N447FE *Shaunna*
HB-IPC	*Schwyz*	217	28.06.83-21.04.95	to Air Liberté as F-GOCJ
HB-IPD	*Solothurn*	260	15.03.84-11.05.95	to FedEx as N448FE *Augustine*
HB-IPE	*Basel-Land*	162	16.12.85-17.03.99	to Air Liberté as F-GPDJ

Boeing 747-300 1983-2000 (5)

400-passenger long-range wide-body aircraft, powered by four 243.5 kN (54,750 lb) Pratt & Whitney JT9D-7R4G2 tuebofan engines, generating a cruising speed of 940 km/h

HB-IGC*	*Bern*	22704/570	19.03.83-30.06.99	to Boeing Capital Corporation (BCC) as N270BC
HB-IGD*	*Basel*	22705/576	05.03.83-25.08.99	to Boeing Capital Corporation (BCC) as N705BC
HB-IGE	*Genève*	22995/585	10.09.92-00.02.00	ex N221GE; wfu, later to South African Airwaus (SAA) as ZS-SKB
HB-IGF	*Zürich*	22996/586	09.09.92-00.06.00	ex N221GF; wfu, later to South African Airways (SAA) as ZS-SKA
HB-IGG*	*Ticino*	23751/686	04.12.87-03.06.99	to FSBU First Security Bank of Utah as N375TC
N221GE	*Genève*	22995/585	16.12.83-10.09.92	reregistered HB-IGE
N221GF	*Zürich*	22996/586	30.11.83-09.09.92	reregistered HB-IGF

* Boeing 747-300 Combi

Fokker 100 HB-IVF

Airbus A310-300 1985-2000 (6)

220-passenger medium/long-range wide-body aircraft, powered by two 222 kN (50,000 lb) Pratt & Whitney JT9D-7R4E1 turbofan engines, generating a cruising speed of 850 km/h

HB-IPF	*Glarus*	399	16.12.85-17.03.99	to Boeing Capital Corporation (BCC) as D-ASRA
HB-IPG	*Zug*	404	20.12.85-11.06.99	to Airbus Financial Services (AFS) as F-WITH
HB-IPH	*Appenzell IR*	409	15.01.86-11.03.99	to Oman Air as A40-OA
HB-IPI	*Luzern*	410	31.01.86-09.04.99	to Oman Air as A40-OB
HB-IPK	*Liestal*	412	01.02.93-08.05.99	taken over from Balair/CTA; to Boeing Capital Corporation (BCC) as D-ASRB
HB-IPN		672	25.01.96-22.03.00	taken over from Balair/CTA; to Airbus Finacial Services (AFS) as F-WIHP

Fokker 100 1988-1996 (10)

107-passenger narrow-bod regional jetliner, powered by two 67.2 kN (15,100 lb) Rolls-Royce Tay Mk.650 -15 turbofan engines, generating a speed of 845 km/h

HB-IVA	*Aarau*	11244	01.03.88-13.11.95	to Alpi Eagles as I-ALPK
HB-IVB	*Biel/Bienne*	11250	21.04.88-25.11.95	to Alpi Eagles as I-ALPL
HB-IVC	*Chur*	11251	01.06.88-24.08.96	to Alpi Eagles as I-ALPX
HB-IVD	*Dietlikon*	11252	14.07.88-01.06.96	to Alpi Eagles as I-ALPZ
HB-IVE	*Baden*	11253	01.08.88-00.00.96	to Royal Brunei Airlines as V8-RB3
HB-IVF	*Sion/Sitten*	11254	16.09.88-02.07.96	to Alpi Eagles as I-ALPS
HB-IVG	*Genthod*	11255	21.10.88-04.10.96	to Royal Brunei Airlines as V8-RB4
HB-IVH	*Stadel*	11256	21.11.88-19.12.96	to Alpi Eagles as I-ALPQ
HB-IVI	*Bellevue*	11381	10.04.92-02.01.96	to Comgnie Corse Méditerranée as F-GKHD
HB-IVK	*Hochfelden*	11386	28.04.92-19.12.96	to Compagnie Corse Méditerranée as F-GKHE

McDonnell Douglas MD-11 1991-2002 (20)

300-passenger long-range wide-body aircraft, powered by three 275 kN (62,000 lb) Pratt & Whitney PW4460 turbofan engines, generating a cruising speed of 900 km/h

HB-IWA	*Obwalden*	48443/458	06.03.91-31.03.02	taken over by SWISS
HB-IWB	*Graubünden*	48444/459	30.03.91-31.03.02	taken over by SWISS
HB-IWC	*Vaud, Schaffhausen*	48445/460	22.04.91-31.03.02	taken over by SWISS
HB-IWD	*Thurgau*	48446/463	30.05.91-31.03.02	taken over by SWISS
HB-IWE	*Nidwalden*	48447/464	14.06.91-31.03.02	taken over by SWISS
HB-IWF	*Schaffhausen, Vaud*	48448/465	05.08.91-02.09.98	crashed near Peggy's Cove, Nova Scotia, Canada
HB-IWG	*Valais/Wallis*	48452/472	19.09.91-31.03.02	SWISSair Asia titles; taken over by SWISS
HB-IWH	*St Gallen*	48453/473	02.10.91-31.03.02	taken over by SWISS
HB-IWI	*Uri*	48454/477	15.11.91-31.03.02	taken over by SWISS

HB-IWK	Fribourg	48455/487	03.02.92-31.03.02	taken over by SWISS
HB-IWL	Appenzell Ausserrhoden	48456/494	13.04.92-31.03.02	SWISSair Asia titles; taken over by SWISS
HB-IWM	Jura	48457/498	01.06.92-31.03.02	taken over by SWISS
HB-IWN		48539/571	29.07.94-31.03.02	SWISSair Asia titles; taken over by SWISS
HB-IWO	Schwyz	48540/611	11.03.97-31.03.02	taken over by SWISS
HB-IWP	Basel Land	48634/614	11.07.97-31.03.02	taken over by SWISS
HB-IWQ	Valais	48541/621	22.12.97-31.03.02	taken over by SWISS
HB-IWR	Bern	48484/484	29.10.98-31.03.02	ex D-AERB; taken over by SWISS
HB-IWS	Ticino	48485/502	05.11.98-31.02.03	ex D-AERW; grounded
HB-IWT	Basel	48486/509	02.11.98-31.03.02	ex D-AERX; grounded
HB-IWU	Luzern	48538/533	27.10.98-31.03.02	ex D-AERZ; grounded

Airbus A321-100 1995-2002 (12)

230-passenger short/medium-range aircraft, powered by two 147 kN (33,000 lb) CFM International CFM56-5B1 turbofan engines, generating a speed of 850 km/h

HB-IOA	Neuchâtel	517	17.05.95-31.03.02	taken over by SWISS
HB-IOB	Aargau	519	14.03.95-31.03.02	taken over by SWISS
HB-IOC	Lausanne	520	07.03.95-31.03.02	taken over by SWISS
HB-IOD	Kloten	522	04.04.95-31.03.02	taken over by SWISS
HB-IOE	Solothurn	535	20.06.95-31.03.02	to Air Méditerrané as F-GAYN via ILFC
HB-IOF	Winterthur	541	11.05.97-31.03.02	taken over by SWISS
HB-IOG	Bülach	642	21.01.97-31.03.02	to Air Méditerrané as F-GAYO via ILFC
HB-IOH	Würenlos	664	21.02.97-31.03.02	taken over by SWISS
HB-IOI	Délemont	827	20.05.98-31.03.02	taken over by SWISS
HB-IOJ	Frauenfeld	891	02.11.98-31.03.02	taken over by SWISS
HB-IOK		987	19.03.99-31.03.02	taken over by SWISS
HB-IOL	Lugano	1144	21.12.99-31.03.02	taken over by SWISS

Airbus A320-200 1995-2002 (20)

150-passenger narrowbody airliner, powered by two 120 kN (27,000 lb) CFM International CFM56-5B4 turbofan engines, generating a speed of 830 km/h

HB-IJA	Opfikon	533	31.05.95-31.03.02	grounded, later to China Northwest Airlines as B-2224
HB-IJB	Embrach	545	29.08.95-31.03.02	grounded, later to Turkish Airlines as TC-JLA Şanliurfa
HB-IJC	Winkel	548	15.09.95-31.03.02	grounded, later to China northwest Airlines as B-2214
HB-IJD	Regensdorf	553	23.10.95-31.03.02	grounded, later to Aer Lingus as EI-CZV
HB-IJE	Dübendorf	559	24.11.95-31.03.02	grounded, later to Aer Lingus as EI-CZW
HB-IJF	Bellevue	562	15.12.95-31.03.02	taken over by SWISS
HB-IJG	Illnau-Effretikon	566	19.01.96-31.03.02	grounded, later to Turkish Airlines as TC-JLC Kahramanmaraş

HB-IJH	Wangen-Brüttisellen	574	29.02.96-31.03.02	grounded, later to Turkish Airlines as TC-JLD Mersin
HB-IJI	Binningen	577	21.03.96-31.03.02	taken over by SWISS
HB-IJJ	Dietlikon	585	10.05.96-31.03.02	taken over by SWISS
HB-IJK	Genthod	596	25.06.96-31.03.02	taken over by SWISS
HB-IJL	Bassersdorf	603	12.07.96-31.03.02	taken over by SWISS
HB-IJM	Wallisellen	635	29.11.96-31.03.02	taken over by SWISS
HB-IJN	Meyrin	643	20.12.96-31.03.02	taken over by SWISS
HB-IJO	Grand-Saconnex	673	25.04.97-31.03.02	taken over by SWISS
HB-IJP	Vernier	681	29.05.97-31.03.02	taken over by SWISS
HB-IJQ	Niederhasli	701	30.06.97-31.03.02	taken over by SWISS
HB-IJR	Air-La-Ville	703	16.07.97-31.03.02	taken over by SWISS
HB-IJS	Neerach	782	24.03.97-31.03.02	taken over by SWISS
HB-IJT	Nürensdorf	870	20.05.99-31.03.02	taken over by SWISS

Airbus A319-100 1996-2002 (10)

125-passenger short/medium-range aircraft, powered by two 120 kN (27,000 lb) CFM International CFM56-5B5 turbofan engines, generating a speed of 850 km/h

HB-IPR	Commune de Champagne	1018	12.05.99-31.03.02	taken over by SWISS
HB-IPS	Weiach	734	22.10.97-31.03.02	taken over by SWISS
HB-IPT	Stadel	727	26.09.97-31.03.02	taken over by SWISS
HB-IPU	Hochfelden	713	30.08.97-31.03.02	taken over by SWISS
HB-IPV	Rümlang	578	25.04.96-31.03.02	taken over by SWISS
HB-IPW	Bachenbülach	588	23.05.96-31.03.02	taken over by SWISS
HB-IPX	Steinmaur	612	23.08.96-31.03.02	taken over by SWISS
HB-IPY	Höri	621	18.10.96-31.03.02	taken over by SWISS
HB-IPZ	Oberglatt	629	19.11.96-31.03.02	grounded, later to Lotus Air as SU-LBF
OO-SSJ		1305	01.09.00-28.10.00	leased from Sabena

Airbus A319-100 still with its French test registration

Airbus A330-200 1998-2002 (16)

250-passenger long-range wide-body aircraft, powered by two 305 kN (68,600 lb) Pratt & Whitney PW4168A turbofan engines, generating a cruising speed of 870 km/h

HB-IQA	*Valais*	229	04.09.98-31.03.02	taken over by SWISS
HB-IQB	*Glarus*	240	11.12.98-31.03.02	taken over by SWISS
HB-IQC	*Zug*	249	11.12.98-31.03.02	taken over by SWISS
HB-IQD	*Liechtenstein*	253	05.02.99-31.03.02	taken over by SWISS
HB-IQE	*Appenzell i. Rh.*	255	19.02.99-31.03.02	taken over by SWISS
HB-IQF	*Bellinzona*	262	12.03.99-31.03.02	taken over by SWISS
HB-IQG		275	26.05.99-31.03.02	taken over by SWISS
HB-IQH	*Chur*	288	20.07.99-31.03.02	taken over by SWISS
HB-IQI	*Liestal*	291	06.08.99-31.03.02	taken over by SWISS
HB-IQJ		294	15.09.99-31.03.02	taken over by SWISS
HB-IQK		299	06.10.99-31.03.02	taken over by SWISS
HB-IQL		305	11.11.00-31.03.02	grounded, later to Lufthansa as D-AIMA
HB-IQM	*Zürich*	308	19.11.99-31.03.02	grounded, later to Lufthansa as D-AIMB
HB-IQN	*Genève*	312	14.12.99-31.03.02	grounded, later to Lufthansa as D-AIMC
HB-IQO		343	23.06.00-31.03.02	taken over by SWISS
HB-IQP		366	22.05.01-31.03.02	taken over by SWISS

Swiss Airbus A330-300 HB-JHC

Schweizerische Luftverkehrsschule (SLS)

Pilatus P-3

Two-seat low-wing cantilever monoplane for primary and advanced training, powered by a single 190 kW (260 hp) Lycoming GO-435 piston engine, generating a maximum speed of 310 km/h (193 mph)

HB-HOE	335	12.08.59-04.04.63	to Brazilian Marine as

Piaggio P.149E

Four-seat low-wing cantilever monoplane for primary training, powered by a single 201 kW (270 hp) Lycoming GO-480 engine, generating a maximum speed of 304 km/h (189 mph)

HB-EBQ	348	29.05.63-30.06.97	
HB-EBV	346	20.04.61-30.06.97	
HB-EBW	347	10.05.61-25.08.70	crashed at Zurich-Altstetten
HB-EEO	349	13.09.65-30.06.97	crashed at Baar
HB-EER	350	23.09.65-30.06.97	

Piaggio P.149D

Four-seat low-wing cantilever monoplane for primary training, powered by a single 201 kW (270 hp) Lycoming GO-480 engine, generating a maximum speed of 304 km/h (189 mph)

HB-EFW	FW102	15.09.70-30.06.97	
HB-EFX	FW266	15.09.70-30.06.97	
HB-EFZ	FW321	15.09.70-30.06.97	
HB-EIQ	FW262	28.02.79-30.06.97	
HB-EJX	FW070	01.04.89-30.06.97	
HB-KIS	FW089	26.06.91-30.06.97	
HB-KIU	FW175	28.05.91-17.09.96	

Douglas C-47B

21-passengers low-wing, all-metal monoplane, powered by two 895 kW (1,200 hp) Pratt & Whitney R-1830-S1C3G Twin Wasp engines, generating a speed of 370 km/h (230 mph)

HB-IRC*	42978	01.04.64-30.04.69	to Protea Airways as ZS-FRJ
HB-IRN	33393	01.04.64-30.04.69	transferred to Transport Museum, Lucerne
HB-IRX	26162	01.04.64-30.04.69	to Ethiopian Airlines as ET-ADC

* Douglas DC-3D

SIAT 223 A1 Flamingo

Three-seat low-wing monoplane for standard training, powered by a single 149 kW (200 hp) Avco-Lycoming IO=360 piston engine, generating a maximum speed of 243 km/h (151 mph)

HB-EVF	11/A1	21.03.68-25.05.83	to Farner Werke, Grenchen
HB-EVG	12/A1	21.03.68-25.05.83	to Farner Werke, Grenchen
HB-EVH	13/A1	29.04.68-07.07.83	to Farner Werke, Grenchen
HB-EVK	14/A1	30.04.68-04.07.83	to Farner Werke, Grenchen
HB-EVL	15/A1	08.05.68-25.05.83	to Farner Werke, Grenchen
HB-EVM	16/A1	14.05.68-07.07.83	to Farner Werke, Grenchen
HB-EVN	17/A1	04.06.68-29.06.83	to Farner Werke, Grenchen

SIAT 223 K1 Flamingo

Single-seat low-wing monoplane for aerobatic training, powered by a single 149 kW (200 hp) Avco-Lycoming IO-360 piston engine, generating a speed of 243 km/h (151 mph)

HB-EVB	18/K1	30.10.68-25.05.83	to Farner Werke, Grenchen
HB-EVC	19/K1	23.01.69-04.03.82	crashed am Hirzel
HB-EVD	20/K1	23.01.69-16.10.82	to Farner Werke, Grenchen

Pilatus PC-7

Tandem-seat low-wing aircraft for basic training, powered by a single 410 kW (550 shp) Pratt & Whitney Canada PT6A-25A turboprop engine, generating a maximum speed of 412 km/h (256 mph)

HB-HOO	394	11.08.92-
HB-HOQ	549	07.07.88-

Pilatus PC-7

Swissair brand through the years

The first 10 years were largely experimental, with no standard approach to presenting a visual uniformity. While the word Swissair was dominant, the lettering varied considerable and also used were Swiss Air, Swiss Air Lines and even Switzerland Air. Aircraft also sported a variety of liveries, including predominantly blue and red or bare metal fuselages, often with the nationality marks of CH- set in red tail units. In the mid-1930s, these crystallised into metal fuselages, with the upper tailfins carrying the Swiss national flag with the inset white cross. The airline logo also soon became standard, with flowing red lettering preceded by an elongated S, and the titles on its aircraft were Swiss Air Lines. During World War Two, some aircraft were painted in special neutrality markings, which comprised broad red and white bands wrapped around the bare metal fuselage at the front and towards the rear.

Once the war had ended, the airline began a major redesign of logo and livery. The logo, designed by Rudi Bircher, comprised a stylized aircraft with an arrow denoting forward speed and the word Swissair, for the first time in capitals, set within, and the design was sometimes surrounded by a red circle. The livery was standardized with an upper white fuselage above bare metal, the two divided

by a double red windowline. The partially red tail with the Swiss cross remained, as did the Swiss Airlines titling. This changed in 1956 with the arrival of the Douglas DC-7C, when a solid red cheatline across the windows was visually more pleasing, and the titles were changed to Swissair.

A major redesign was implemented 25 years later with the arrival of the McDonnell Douglas MD-81 in 1981. The red cheatline was replaced by twin lines in two different shades of brown. While the allusion to Swiss chocolate is tempting, the real rationale for this change has never been published. The tail unit was now completely covered in red. The new logo now featured a bolder Swissair name in black, all lower case, alongside a bevelled rectangle, unambiguously representing the Swiss flag. The cheatline was dropped in 1995 and, starting with the delivery of the Airbus A320 family, aircraft now flew in snow white, with a grey belly. After Swissair joined the Qualiflyer Alliance, some aircraft in the fleet were given a blue belly, with the exception of the Airbus A319-100.

The SAir Group was founded as a holding company for Swissair and affiliates on 22 May 1997, which had their own distinctive logos

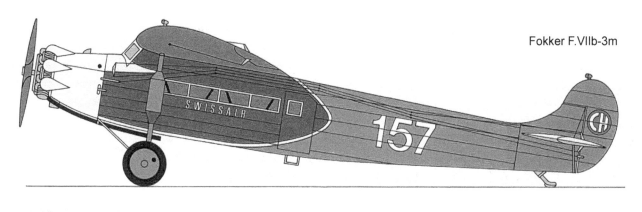

Fokker F.VIIb-3m

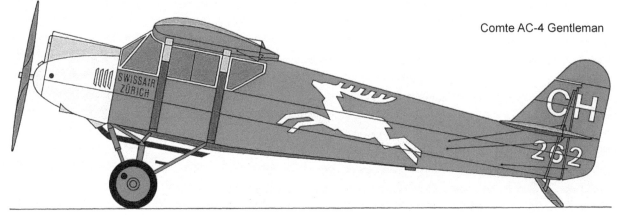

Comte AC-4 Gentleman

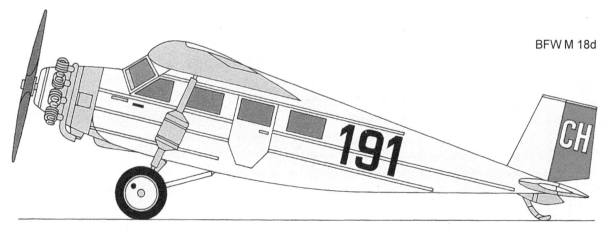

BFW M 18d

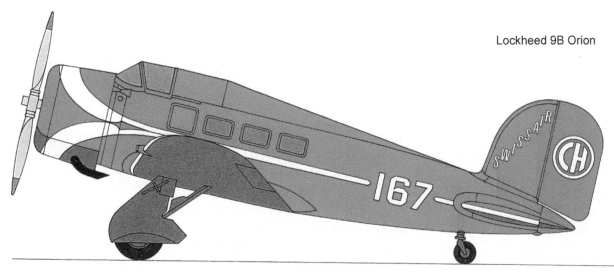

Lockheed 9B Orion

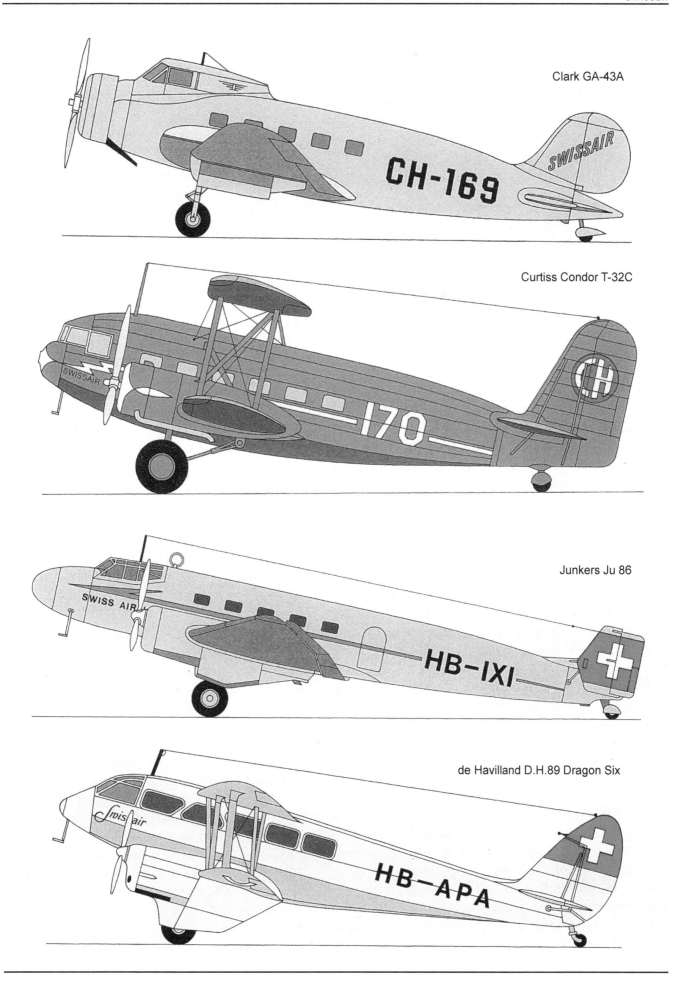

Clark GA-43A

Curtiss Condor T-32C

Junkers Ju 86

de Havilland D.H.89 Dragon Six

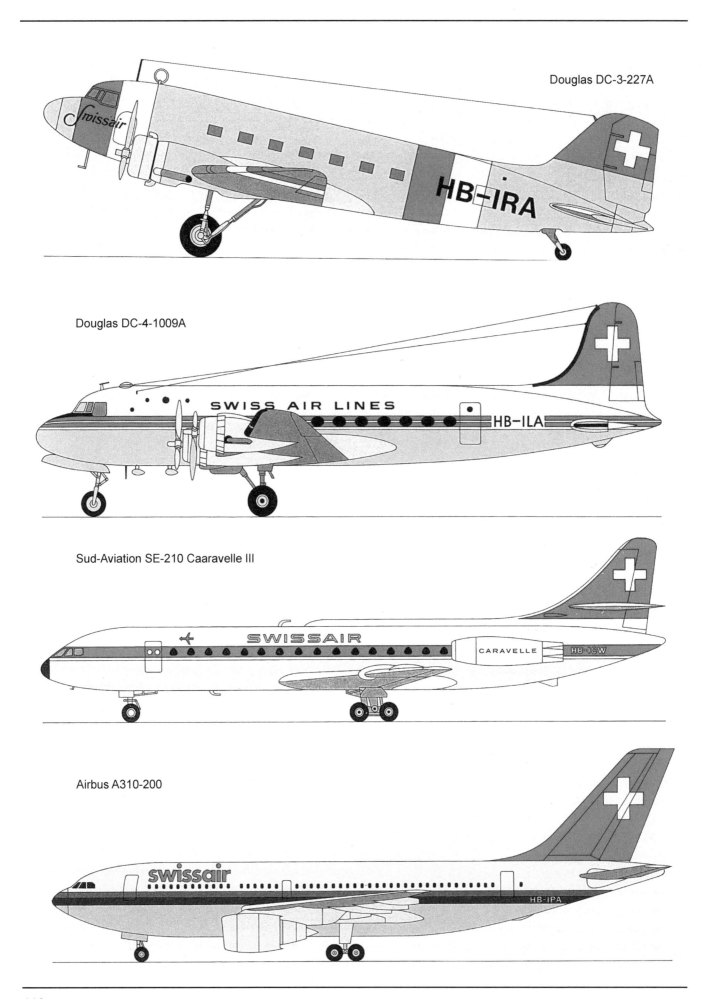

Douglas DC-3-227A

HB-IRA

Douglas DC-4-1009A

SWISS AIR LINES

HB-ILA

Sud-Aviation SE-210 Caaravelle III

SWISSAIR

CARAVELLE

HB-ICW

Airbus A310-200

swissair

HB-IPA

Crossair

From a modest start operating small aircraft for hire, training and air-taxi work, Crossair's enthusiastic and dynamic management developed the company into one of Europe's biggest regional airlines, in part with the acquiescence and financial participation of Swissair. That it would eventually succeed its bigger partner as Switzerland's national airline was a future never envisaged

On 14 February 1975, Moritz Suter, then a DC-9 captain with Swissair, and his friend, Peter Kalt, established Business Flyers Basle AG with a capital of CHF 65,000. With a fleet of one Cessna 310P, HB-LFK, with accommodation for four passengers, and an aged two-seat Piper L-4 Cub, HB-OJC, it offered mainly aircraft leasing and air-taxi flights, operating the first commercial flight on 1 November 1976. In the same year, the capital was increased to CHF 165,000. More Cessna aircraft, including a twin-engined Cessna 551 Citation jet, HB-VGE, boosted the fleet over the next two years. But Suter's ambitions lay beyond the limitations of air-taxi work. Deregulation in the United States, which spawned many new commuter airlines, and tentative moves to open up the restrictive European market, encouraged him to formulate a plan for a regional airline that would serve smaller communities within Switzerland and neighbouring countries, destinations which Swissair could not serve with its larger prop and jet aircraft. Swissair's management initially expressed an interest in taking a 40 per cent stake, but it suddenly withdrew its promise of co-operation and financial participation, but by then Suter had already taken steps and had crossed the point of no return.

He changed the name to Crossair AG on 18 November 1978, increased the capital to CHF 1million. and applied

Moritz Suter

for traffic rights from Zurich to Lyon, Luxembourg, Nuremberg, Innsbruck, Klagenfurt and Lugano. In anticipation of being successful in its application, at least in part, Crossair signed options for four Swearingen SA.226-TC Metro II, a 19-seat pressurised airliner, powered by two 750 kW (1,000 hp) Garrett AiResearch TPE-331 turboprop engines, and with a range was 1,100 km. On 26 April 1979, the *Eidgenössische Luftamt* (Federal Air Office) granted a provisional operator's certificate for scheduled flights from Zurich to Nuremberg, Innsbruck

HB-LLB was one of three Fairchild Swearingen Metro II aircraft in the early Crossair fleet

The Metro fleet was soon boosted by the upgraded Metro III with deliveries starting in May 1981

and Klagenfurt, enabling Crossair to firm up its order for the Metro II. The first aircraft, HB-LLA, was delivered on 30 May 1979, and started services to the three destinations on 2 July. In the first full year of operation in 1980, Crossair carried 50,237 passengers and 37,000 kg of freight.

That same year, the network was increased with new services from Zurich to Hanover and Düsseldorf, Zurich and Geneva to Turin, and from Berne to Paris. The Italian authorities granted a concession for a Lugano-Venice service. Lugano was also connected to Zurich and Geneva. Rotterdam and Maastricht were added from Zurich the following year. An order was placed on 27 March for four upgraded SA.227-AC Metro III, later increased to nine, and, in October 1980, Crossair became the launch customer for the Saab/Fairchild SF340, a 33-seat twin-turboprop regional airliner, which it named *Cityliner*, with an order for 10 aircraft, marking a significant step-up in capacity. To finance the new aircraft, the capital was increased to CHF 16 million.

Crossair's rapid growth, facilitated by a positive bottom-line, caught the attention of Swissair, which was determined to put the upstart in its place. On 31 December 1981, it applied for traffic rights on the routes served by Crossair, taking advantage of its monopoly position under Swiss law, even though it did not have suitable aircraft to operate these secondary services. Swissair, therefore, contracted German airline DLT to operate on its behalf. However, Swissair did not reckon with the outcry from customers and the media, who objected strongly about the shabby treatment of the young airline. The whole affair became political and a compromise was reached in February 1982 for closer co-operation, that appeared to satisfy both airlines. While Swissair was given the traffic rights, Crossair was allowed to operate flights out of Basle-Mulhouse, which was a great boost to the Basle region, and took over some of Swissair's loss-making routes.

The first routes out of Basle served Geneva, Zurich, Brussels, Munich and Vienna, and Crossair also replaced Swissair on the services from Basle to Paris and Frankfurt. The European Council Directive of 25 July 1983, concerning the liberalisation of regional air traffic, which limited such services to Category 2 airports, was a first tentative, but not universally appreciated step towards full deregulation but had little effect on Crossair's operation. Crossair was granted a full operator's certificate by the Swiss Federal Air Office in November that year, and preparations were made for the introduction of the Saab-Fairchild SF340A, the first of which, HB-AHA, was delivered on 6 June 1984 and made its first flight on 12 June carrying Pope John Paul II to Lugano. The new type was then put onto a twice-daily Basle-Paris service, replacing Swissair's loss-making DC-9 flight, and also took over from the Metro III on other busy routes. In the meantime, the capital had been increased first to CHF 25 million, and then doubled to CHF 50 million.

Growth continued unabated. While initial relations with Swissair were merely lukewarm, based on the David versus Goliath principle, a new unlimited co-operation contract was signed in 1986, which guaranteed Crossair's existing network flown with aircraft up to 40-seat capacity. A contract with DLH gave Crossair an entry into the cargo business, opening a night cargo flight between Basle and Brussels. On 5 May 1986, for the first time in Swiss history, a flight was operated with an all-female crew between Basle and Munich. The last Metro III was sold the following year, and the Saab 340A fleet was further increased and eventually numbered 35, including six 340AF modified freighters and 18 of the improved 340B, which differed very little externally, but its more powerful CT7-9B engines provided improved hot-and-high performance, while the range was also increased to 1,300 km. The first

The higher-capacity Saab 340A marked a major step-up in capacity

Line-up of 10 Saab 340A and 340B twin-turboprop regional airliners

A special scheme on Saab 340A HB-AHD designed by 10-year-old Giacomo Fiscalini celebrated the 700th anniversary of the Swiss Federation

Saab 340A HB-AHS in the new livery

340B, HB-AKA, was delivered on 15 September 1989.

Traffic forecasts convinced Crossair that it needed a larger, 50-seat aircraft, if it was to keep pace with expected development. It persuaded Saab to build a stretched version of the 340 and the project was approved in December 1988 with the support of a launch order from Crossair for 25 aircraft. The new Saab 2000, named *Concordino* by Crossair, was officially launched in May 1989. As an interim measure while awaiting the Saab 2000, Crossair agreed, with little enthusiasm, to obtain five 46-seat Fokker 50 twin-turboprop aircraft, which were intended to replace Swissair's larger Fokker 100

on the Geneva-Luxembourg and Zurich-Genoa routes, and on sectors to Nuremberg, Salzburg, Stuttgart and Turin. It also placed an order for four British Aerospace 146-200 four-engined jets for its growing European market, but had to overcome objections from Swissair, as the 146 would be a direct competitor to the Fokker 100. Swissair cemented its arrangement with Crossair by acquiring a 38 per cent stake, with 41 per cent voting rights, soon acquiring a majority holding of 70.2 per cent. The capital had been further increased to CHF 215 million, but 1989 ended with a first loss of CHF 6.7 million, as the aviation industry found itself in crisis

The Fokker 50 was an interim measure pending delivery of the Saab 2000

The 16-strong four-engine British Aerospace RJ100 fleet included HB-IXU and HB-IXW

Regional collaboration

Expanding its coverage of Europe was the priority for Crossair. For this reason, it invested in several smaller regional airlines that offered connecting services to destinations Crossair itself could not reach. All were provided with a Saab 340A or 340B, which were no longer needed for its own fleet. Business Air Ltd was founded at Aberdeen, Scotland by Graeme Ross and Ian Woodley on 14 May 1987 and developed a small network from Aberdeen to Manchester, Dundee and Esbjerg, and also briefly operated a Belfast-Manchester link. It was acquired by British Midland Airways in April 1996. Germany's Delta Air Regionalfluggesellschaft was founded on 1 April 1978 and provided services from Bodensee-Airport Friedrichshafen on Lake Constance to Zurich and Stuttgart, later adding flights to Bremen, Frankfurt, Cologne/Bonn and Berlin/Tempelhof. It was bought by British Airways and German banks in May 1992 and was renamed Deutsche BA. Crossair established Tatra Air in a joint venture with Slov-Air, based at Bratislava/Ivanka in Slovakia, which started operations on 28 March 1991 to Zurich and Munich, but sold its stake to Slov-Air in 1992. French regional Alsavia, like Crossair, was based at Basle. It was founded on 22 February 1989 by André-Paul Weber, and started operations in October on behalf of Air France, which later took a 14 per cent shareholding. TAT (Touraine Air Transport) acquired 20 per cent and Crossair 33.33 per cent. The only schedule operated was between Basle-Mulhouse and Marseille. It filed for bankruptcy on 3 February 1993. Surplus Swearingen Metro aircraft were handed to

another associate, short-lived Cargo and Passenger Air Services AG (CPS), which started operations in 1986 It provided feeder services for major courier companies and postal authorities to Brussels and Maastricht from Milan/Bergamo, Geneva and EuroAirport Basle-Mulhouse-Freiburg. In October 1997, Crossair set up a new company in the Alsace region of France under French law, to take advantage of airline liberalisation in the European Union and to strengthen its Basle hub. Crossair provided 40 per cent of the FFR 20 million (USD 3.4 million) share capital, with the remaining 60 per cent provided by French and German companies. Operations began from the Basle airport on 29 March 1998 under the name of Crossair Europe (European Continental Airways) using two Saab 340B airliners, F-GPKD (ex HB-AKD), and F-GPKG (ex HB-AKG). A third, F-GPKM (ex HB-AKM), was added later. Initial routes out of Basle served Milan/Malpensa, Venice and Marseille, with other destinations added subsequently. Operations ceased on 28 March 2005.

Crossair shareholdings in other regional airlines

Alsavia	33.33%	1989-1993
Business Air	40.00%	1987-1996
CPS	33.33%	1986-
Crossair Europe	40.00%	1997-2005
Delta Air	40.00%	1982-1992
Tatra Air	50.00%	1991-1992

The first Fokker 50, HB-IAN, was delivered on 8 May 1990, and entered service on 21 May. Two more arrived before the end of the year, with the remaining two in 1991. Also introduced in 1990 were three BAe 146-200, although these were second-hand aircraft from USAir, as the manufacturer was unable to deliver new aircraft in time. Crossair took delivery of the first, HB-IXB, on 17 May, and put it into service on 18 June on the Basle-Amsterdam and Basle-Munich routes in an 84-seat configuration. The second aircraft, HB-IXC, took over the service between Geneva, Zurich, Lugano and Venice. HB-IXB carried the name *Il folletto silencioso de Lugano* (the quiet little bird from Lugano). The 146 was a short-range, high-wing monoplane with four 31.1 kN (6,990 lb) Lycoming ALF 502R-5 turbofan engines

mounted on pylons under the wing. Crossair also acquired four Avro RJ 85, an improved version of the 146-200 with more efficient Honeywell LF 507 engines, and two stretched 146-300 variants. With the increased fleet, Crossair was able to carry 1 million passengers for the first time in 1990.

The aftermath of the Gulf War and the weak world economy continued to affect operations and resulted in another loss in 1991. However, the network was further expanded with new services from Zurich to Dresden and Leipzig, and from Basle to London and Barcelona, now including 34 destinations in 10 countries. Some 30 per cent of flights were conducted on behalf of Swissair. A small profit of CHF1.1 million was achieved in 1992, in part through the sale of its 40 per cent stake in German

Crossair's first British Aerospace RJ85 HB-IXF was delivered on 23 April 1993

Saab 2000 HB-IZJ was one of 34 of the type in the Crossair fleet

regional Delta Air on 20 March. London City Airport was serviced for the first time from Zurich, and Crossair also took over the Basle-London/Heathrow service from its parent company. On 2 April 1993, Crossair introduced a new logo, and took delivery of its first RJ85, HB-IXF, on 23 April. It named the type *Jumbolino*. Receipts from the sale of aircraft and financial transactions, as well as an extended cooperation with Swissair, contributed to a record net profit of CHF 24.1 million. Another reason for the good result was the increase in passenger load factor to 53 per cent, an improvement that was maintained in 1994.

The route network was greatly expanded with new services to Birmingham, Dublin, Hanover, Copenhagen, Marseille and Toulouse, and progress was made in holiday charter flights. At the same time, the short-range charter segment of Balair/CTA was transferred to Crossair in March 1994. Plans were being made for large-scale expansion, starting with Crossair being charged by Swissair to take over all scheduled services with aircraft up to 100 seats. A major element of the proposed expansion was

Saab 2000 HB-IZK with special Phantom of the Opera livery

Special paint scheme on Saab 2000 HB-IYD highlighting Sion's bid for the 2006 Winter Olympics

the delivery of a large fleet of the Saab 2000 *Concordino*. The first aircraft, HB-IZC, entered service in September 1994. A high-speed turboprop airliner, powered by two AE 2100P turboprop engines generating a cruise speed of 665 km/h, the Saab 2000 was capable of operating over short- and medium-range routes with similar block times to jet aircraft, yet retaining the efficiency produced by turboprop engines. The first six aircraft were delivered with a mechanical elevator control system (MECS), but a hydraulic powered elevator control system (PECS) was later installed in these and subsequent aircraft. Crossair's Saab 2000 fleet eventually reached 34 units.

McDonnell Douglas MD-82 HB-INV was taken over from Swissair

McDonnell Douglas MD-83 twinjet HB-IUH in McDonnald's colours in association with Hotelplan

Saab 2000 in Euro Cross markings

Further fleet expansion was implemented with an order for 12 Avro RJ100 jets, to replace Swissair's Fokker 100, authorised on 29 March 1995. First delivery of HB-, took place already on 19 October, The RJ100 was improved variant of the 146-300. On 29 October, Crossair opened services to Seville and Las Palmas de Gran Canaria. Upon the closure of Balair/CTA, Crossair took over two McDonnell Douglas MD-80 twinjets for its short-range charter business, as well as two more from Swissair. To facilitate the growth spurt, shareholders authorised an increase in capital to CHF328.5 million. Significant net profits were achieved over the next five years. On 31 January 1996, Crossair sold its stake in Scottish airline Business Air. One MD-83,

HB-IUH, entered service on 1 April 1996 in the colours of McDonald's, as part of a promotion with travel company Hotelplan. The EuroCross hub system at EuroAirport Basle-Mulhouse-Freiburg was further strengthened. With the restructuring at Swissair, Crossair became part of SAirLines and, in summer 1998, a member of the Qualiflyer Group and its frequent flyer programme. The year ended with a 14.9 per cent increase in revenues to CHF 1.1 billion, and a net profit up 47.1 per cent to CHF 26.9 million. Annual passenger numbers also improved considerably to 5.4 million.

As replacement for the Saab and Avro fleets, Crossair, having ruled out products from Bombardier and Dornier, placed a massive order for 200 new Embraer twinjets at the

British Aerospace RJ100 HB-IXR in the final Crossair livery

Paris Air Show on 15 June 1999. The order comprised 25 45-seat ERJ145, plus 15 options; 30 70-seat ERJ170, plus 50 options; and 30 108-seat ERJ190-200 twinjets, plus 50 options. It thus became the launch customer for the ERJ170 and ERJ190, but never accepted delivery. However, it took delivery of 22 of the 25 ERJ145, the first, HB-JAA, arriving in Switzerland on 4 March 2000. Crossair operated both the ERJ145LR, a long-range version with increased fuel capacity and upgraded engines, and the ERJ145LU, similar but with increased take-off weight. Its 25th Anniversary since its foundation, however, started with a tragic accident, its first, when Saab 340B, HB-AKK, crashed two minutes after take-off in the Swiss municipality of Niederhasli on a flight from Zurich to Dresden on 10 January 2000. The three crew members and the seven passengers lost their lives. Increased fuel prices, the strength of the US dollar, and the loss of the charter business, which had reverted to

the re-established BalairCTA, plunged Crossair into a CHF 28 million loss and forced it to scale back its growth plans.

As it turned out, Crossair did not have any choice in the matter, as it suffered a turbulent year due to the financial instability of the SAir Group. To make matter worse, on a flight from Berlin/Tegel to Zurich, the Avro RJ100, HB-IXM, crashed on approach in poor visibility into a wooded range of hills near Bassersdorf on 21 November 2001, killing 24 of the 33 people on board. The aircraft broke apart and went up in flames. On 5 October, Crossair had taken over all Swissair's European services and, when Swissair finally ceased operations on 31 March 2002, now owned by UBS, Credit Suisse, the Swiss Confederation and cantons and communities, Crossair started operations as SWISS International Air Lines, SWISS for short, taking over Swissair's intercontinental routes, and most aircraft and assets.

The order for a potential 200 Embraer regional jets never materialised but Crossair took delivery of 22 ERJ45

Crossair Fleet 1978-2002

Fairchild Swearingen SA-226TC Metro II 1979-1985 (3)

19-passenger commuter aircraft, powered by two 701 kW (940 hp) Garrett AiResearch TPE331 turboprop engines, generating a cruising speed of 475 km/h

HB-LLA	TC-291	30.05.79-	
HB-LLB	TC-297	26.07.79-12.04.85	damaged beyond repair on landing at Freidrichshafen, Germany
HB-LLC	TC-330	00/04.80-00.08.82	to Magnum Airlines as ZS-LJC

Fairchild Swearingen SA-227AC Metro III 1981-1990 (9)

19-passenger commuter aircraft, powered by two 745 kW (1,000 hp) Garrett AiResearch TPE-331 turboprop engines, generating a cruising speed of 515 km/h

HB-LLD	AC-425	27.05.81-00.08.85	to Air Cargo Spain as EC-DXT
HB-LLE	AC-429	25.07.81-	
HB-LLF	AC-445	09.09.81-00.10.87	to Delta Connection as N445AC
HB-LNA	AC-448	17.08.81-00.07.87	to Comair as N448CA
HB-LNB	AC-470	18.12.81-00.04.87	to GPA Group
HB-LNC	AC-516	29.04.82-10.06.87	to Ratioflug as D-CFEP
HB-LND	AC-505B	17.04.82-00.04.88	leased to Air Catalunya as EC=DXS 08.85-12.86
HB-LNE	AC-519	11.05.82-00.04.88	to Cargo and Passenger Air Services (CPS) as HB-LNE
HB-LNO	AC-537	27.12.82-12.01.90	to Air Vendee as F-GHVD

Saab 340A 1984-1997 (20)

33-passenger regional aircraft, powered by two 1.294 kW (1,735 hp) General Electric CT7-5A2 turboprop engines, generating a cruising speed of 465 km/h

HB-AHA	5		
HB-AHB*	7	01.07.84-26.07.93	to Business Air as HB-AHB
HB-AHC	9	28.10.84-30.05.96	to Raslan Air Service as SU-PAB
HB-AHD	18	12.03.85-02.04.96	lsd to Delta Air 25.03 to 05.04.90; lsd to Business Air 11.03-21.03.95; to Air Ostrava as OK-PEP
HB-AHE	20	27.03.85-25.09.92	lsd to Tatra Air as OK-RGS; to Business Air as G-GNTC
HB-AHF*	26	20.06.85-01.12.97	lsd to Delta Air/Deutsche BA as D-CDIE 27.12.89-18.02.97; to Hazelton Airlines as VH-ZLY
HB-AHG	38	01.11.85-31.10.97	lsd to Delta Air/Deutsche BA as D-CDIF 01.04.90-01.06.96; to Hazelton Airlines as VH-ZLZ
HB-AHH	40	01.12.85-07.07.95	lsd to Delta Air/Deutsche BA as D-CDIG 16.04.91- ; to Chautauqua Airlines as N40CQ
HB-AHI	43	07.01.86-07.06.95	lsd to Delta Air/Deutsche BA as D-CDIH 01.04.91- ; to Chautauqua Airlines as N43CQ

HB-AHK	49	19.03.86-30.03.91	to British Midland Airways as G-GNTA
HB-AHL*	82	06.03.87-01.09.90	to Business Air as G-GNTB
HB-AHM	84	08.04.87-13.03.92	to Air Nelson as ZK-NSK
HB-AHN	88	30.04.87-27.11.90	to Air Nelson as ZK-FXD
HB-AHO*	113	19.02.88-27.10.94	to Business Air as G-GNTF
HB-AHP	120	01.06.88-16.10.90	to Air Nelson as ZK-FXA
HB-AHQ	122	23.06.88-20.09.90	to Air Nelson as ZK-FXB
HB-AHR*	126	01.08.88-01.10-94	lsd to Swedair as HB-AHR 29.05-26.06.90; to Business Air as G-GNTG
HB-AHS	132	09.11.88-22.02.96	lsd to Business Air as HB-AHS 28.06-16.07.92; to Prima Air as EC-229
HB-AHT	134	01.12.88-23.02.96	to Air Nelson as ZK-NLS
LN-NVD*	37	01.05.88-24.02.89	lsd from Norving

* Saab 340AF

Saab 340B 1989-2002 (15)

33-passenger regional aircraft, powered by two 1,395 kW (1,870 hp) General Electric CT7-9B turboprop engines, generating a cruising speed of 325 km/h

HB-AKA	160	15.09.89-03.08.01	to Moldavian Airlines as ER-SGC
HB-AKB	161	29.09.89-04.04.01	to Aerolitoral as XA-AEM
HB-AKC	164	25.10.89-01.01.01	to Aerolitoral as XA-AEO
HB-AKD	173	29.12.89-01.02.98	to Crossair Europe as F-GPKD
HB-AKE	176	01.02.90-01.07.01	to Aerolitoral as XA-AFR
HB-AKF	182	04.05.90-08.10.00	to Moldavian Airlines as ER-SGB
HB-AKG	185	06.04.90-27.03.98	to Crossair Europe as F-GPKG
HB-AKH	200	18.08.90-01.04.00	to Carpatair as VR-VGN
HB-AKI	208	18.10.90-08.04/00	to Carpatair as YR-VGM
HB-AKK	213	00.11.90-10.01.00	crashed near Niederhasl due to loss of control after take-off from Zurich
HB-AKL	215	07.12.90-29.05.02	lsd to Nordic Airlink as HB-AKL 01.10.-27.12.2000; to Carpatair as YR-VGO
HB-AKM	221	18.01.91-00.04.02	to Crossair Europe as F-GPKM
HB-AKN	225	08.02.91-25.09.01	
HB-AKO	228	02.03.91-07.07.02	to Carpatair as YR-VGP
HB-AKP	168	09.04.91-24.02.97	ex F-GKLA; to Moldavian Airlines as ER-ASA

Fokker 50 1990-1995 (5)

56-passenger short-range aircraft, powered by two1,864 kW (2,500 hp) Pratt & Whitney Canada PW125B turborop engines, generating a cruising speed of 500 km/h

HB-IAN	20182	08.05.90- 20.10.95	to TAM Linhas Aéreas as PT-MLA

HB-IAO	20192	14.09.90-13.11.95	to TAM Linhas Aéreas as PT-MLB
HB-IAP	20202	19.12.90-17.11.95	to TAM Linhas Aéreas as PT-MLC
HB-IAR	20210	21.03.91-16.12.95	to TAM Linhas Aéreas as PT-MLD
HB-IAS	20220	02.07.91-21.12.95	to TAM Linhas Aéreas as PT-MLE

British Aerospace 146-200 1990-1994 (3)

112-passenger short-range high-wing regional jet aircraft, powered by four 31.1 kN (6,990 lb) Lycoming ALF 502R-5 turbofan engines, generating a cruising speed of 747 km/h

HB-IXB	2036	17.05.90-24.08.93	ex N175US; to Business Air as HB-IXB, later G-GNTZ
HB-IXC	2072	17.06.90-08.01.94	ex N190US; to CityJet as EI-CTY
HB-IXD	2073	13.08.90-03.12.93	ex N191US; to BAe as G-BVFV

British Aerospace BAe 146-300 1991-1996 (2)

122-passenger short-range high-wing regional jet aircraft, powered by four 31.1 kN (6,990 lb) Lycoming ALF 502R-5 turbofan engines, generating a cruising speed of 747 km/h

HB-IXY	3163	31.03.94-22.03.96	ex G-BTJG; to Eurowings as D-AEWA
HB-IXZ	3118	18.09.91-22.04.96	to Hamburg Airlines as D-AQUA

British Aerospace RJ85 1993-2002 (4)

112-passenger short-range high-wing regional jet aircraft, powered by four 31.1 kN (6,990 lb) Honeywell LF 507-1F trubofan engines, generating a cruising speed of 747 km/h

HB-IXF	2226	23.04.93-31.03.02	to Swiss International Air Lines
HB-IXG	2231	13.05.93-31.03.02	to Swiss International Air Lines
HB-IXH	2233	26.06.93-31.03.02	to Swiss International Air Lines
HB-IXK	2235	10.07.93-31.03.02	to Swiss International Air Lines

British Aerospace RJ100 1995-2002 (16)

100-passenger high-wing regional jet airliner, powered by four 31.1 kN (6,990 lbf) Honeywell LF 507-1F turbofan engines, generating a maximum speed of 789 km/h

HB-IXM*	3291	23.08.96-24.11.01	crashed near Bassersdorf, Switzerland
HB-IXN	3286	22.07.96-31.03.02	to Swiss International Air Lines
HB-IXO	3284	27.05.96-31.03.02	to Swiss International Air Lines
HB-IXP	3284	27.05.96-31.03.02	to Swiss International Air Lines
HB-IXQ	3282	27.03.96-31,03,02	to Swiss International Air Lines
HB-IXR	3281	29.02.96-31.03.02	to Swiss International Air Lines
HB-IXS	3280	08.02.96-31.03.02	to Swiss International Air Lines
HB-IXT	3259	09.01.96-31.03.02	to Swiss International Air Lines
HB-IXU	3276	22.12.95-31.03.02	to Swiss International Air Lines
HB-IXV	3274	23.11.95-31.03.02	to Swiss International Air Lines

...

HB-IXW	3272	01.11.95-31.03.02	to Swiss International Air Lines
HB-IXX	3262	19.10.95-31.03.02	to Swiss International Air Lines
HB-IYW	3359	08.10.99-31.03.02	to Swiss International Air Lines
HB-IYX	3357	06.09.99-31.03.02	to Swiss International Air Lines
HB-IYY	3339	21.12.98-31.03.02	to Swiss International Air Lines
HB-IYZ	3338	24.11.98-31.03.02	to Swiss International Air Lines

* HB-IXM crashed on approach to Zurich/Kloten on scheduled flight from Berlin/Tegel on 24 November 2001. Three crew and 21 passengers of the 33 occupants lost their life. The aircraft flew controlled into a wooded range of hills because the pilot descended below the mininmum descent altitude of the standard VOR/DME approach without having the required visual contact to the appraoch lights or the runway. The go around initiated proved too late.

Saab 2000 1994-2002 (34)

50-passenger high-speed regional airliner, powered by two 3,096 kW 4.152 hp) Rolls-Royce AE 2100A turboprop engines, generating a cruising speed of 665 km/h

HB-IZA	4	29.09.95-31.03.02	to Swiss International Air Lines
HB-IZB	5	26.10.94-31.03.02	to Swiss International Air Lines
HB-IZC	6	30.08.94-31.03.02	to Swiss International Air Lines
HB-IZD	7	30.09.94-31.03.02	to Swiss International Air Lines
HB-IZE	8	26.09.94-31.03.02	to Swiss International Air Lines
HB-IZF	9	31.10.94-31.03.02	to Swiss International Air Lines
HB-IZG	10	30.01.95-31.03.02	to Swiss International Air Lines
HB-IZH	11	28.02.95-31.03.02	to Swiss International Air Lines
HB-IZI	12	01.04.95-31.03.02	to Swiss International Air Lines
HB-IZJ	15	26.04.95-31.03.02	to Swiss International Air Lines
HB-IZK	18	30.06.95-31.03.02	to Swiss International Air Lines
HB-IZL	22	16.09.95-31.03.02	to Swiss International Air Lines
HB-IZM	24	27.10.95-31.03.02	to Swiss International Air Lines
HB-IZN	26	22.12.95-31.03.02	to Swiss International Air Lines
HB-IZO	29	15.12.95-31.03.02	to Swiss International Air Lines
HB-IZP	31	22.02.96-28.09.01	to Golden Air as SE-LOG
HB-IZQ	32	29.02.96-11.04.02	to Lithuanian Airlines as LY-SBG
HB-IZR	33	21.03.96-31.03.02	to Swiss International Air Lines
HB-IZS	35	19.04.96-31.03.02	lsd to Air One as HB-IZS 03.11.98-15.12.99; to Swiss International Air Lines
HB-IZT	36	30.04.96-31.03.02	to Swiss International Air Lines
HB-IZU	37	31.05.96-31.03.02	to Swiss International Air Lines
HB-IZV	38	09.08.96-31.03.02	to Swiss International Air Lines
HB-IZW	39	20.10.96-31.03.02	to Swiss International Air Lines
HB-IZX	41	24.11.96-31.03.02	to Swiss International Air Lines
HB-IZY	47	29.05.97-31.03.02	to Swiss International Air Lines
HB-IZZ	48	26.06.97-31.03.02	to Swiss International Air Lines
HB-IYA	56	29.04.98-31.03.02	to Swiss International Air Lines

HB-IYB	57	25.06.98-31.03.02	to Swiss International Air Lines
HB-IYC	58	17.09.98-31.03.02	to Swiss International Air Lines
HB-IYD	59	03.11.98-31.03.02	to Swiss International Air Lines
HB-IYE	60	12.02.99-31.03.02	to Swiss International Air Lines
HB-IYF	61	16.04.99-31.03.02	to Swiss International Air Lines
HB-IYG	62	14.04.99-31.03.02	to Swiss International Air Lines
HB-IYH	63	29.04.99-31.03.02	to Swiss International Air Lines

McDonnell Douglas MD-83 1995-2002 (12 MD-81)

172-seat short/medium-range aircraft, powered by two rear-mounted 93kN Pratt & Whitney JT8D-219 turbofan engines, generating a speed of 875km/h

HB-INR*	49277/1181	19.12.95-24.02.01	ex Balair/Swissair; to Nordic Airlink as HB-INR
HB-INV**	49359/1349	31.10.95-25.02.02	ex Swissair; to Odette Airways as HB-INV
HB-INW	49569/1405	05.11.95-10.05.01	ex Balair; to Spantax as EC-HVC
HB-INZ**	49572/1468	27.10.95-24.05.01	ex Swissair; to Spantax as EC-HVX
HB-ISX	49844/1579	21.04.96-30.03.02	ex Swissair; to Swiss International Air Lines
HB-ISZ	49930/1720	02.11.95-30.03.02	ex Balair; to Swiss International Air Lines
HB-IUG	53149/1817	01.02.96-30.03.02	ex Swissair; to Swiss International Air Lines
HB-IUH	53150/1831	01.03.96-30.03.02	ex Swissair; to Swiss International Air Lines
HB-IUM	49847/1585	12.11.97-30.03.02	ex Aero Lloyd D-AGWC; to Swiss International Air Lines
HB-IUN	49769/1559	20.02.98-30.03.02	ex Aero Lloyd D-ALLK; to Swiss International Air Lines
HB-IUO	49857/1687	24.05.98-30.03.02	ex Aero Lloyd D-ALLN; to Swiss International Air Lines
HB-IUP	49856/1675	23.03.99-30.03.02	ex Aero Lloyd D-ALLM; to Swiss International Air Lines

* MD-81
** MD-82

Embraer ERJ145LU 2000-2002 (22)

50-passenger short-range regional jet aircraft, powered by two rear-mounted 33.1 kN (7,440 lb) Rolls-Royce AE 3007-A1 turbofan engines, generating a maximum speed of 833 km/h

HB-JAA	232	04.03.00-31.03.02	to Swiss International Air Lines
HB-JAB	240	23.03.00-31.03.02	to Swiss International Air Lines
HB-JAC	255	28.04.00-31.03.02	to Swiss International Air Lines
HB-JAD*	269	31.05.00-31.03.02	to Swiss International Air Lines
HB-JAE*	281	29.06.00-31.03.02	to Swiss International Air Lines
HB-JAF	313	06.09.00-31.03.02	to Swiss International Air Lines
HB-JAG*	321	27.09.00-31.03.02	to Swiss International Air Lines
HB-JAH	341	16.11.00-31.03.02	to Swiss International Air Lines
HB-JAI	351	07.12.00-31.03.02	to Swiss International Air Lines
HB-JAJ*	382	08.02.01-31.03.02	to Swiss International Air Lines

HB-JAK*	387	22.02.01-31.03.02	to Swiss International Air Lines
HB-JAL	400	22.03.01-31.03.02	to Swiss International Air Lines
HB-JAM	420	20.04.01-31.03.02	to Swiss International Air Lines
HB-JAN	434	22.05.01-31.03.02	to Swiss International Air Lines
HB-JAO	456	29.06.01-31.03.02	to Swiss International Air Lines
HB-JAP	475	27.07.01-31.03.02	to Swiss International Air Lines
HB-JAQ	498	20.09.01-31.03.02	to Swiss International Air Lines
HB-JAR	510	27.09.01-31.03.02	to Swiss International Air Lines
HB-JAS	559	31.01.02-31.03.02	to Swiss International Air Lines
HB-JAT*	564	21.02.02-31.03.02	to Swiss International Air Lines
HB-JAU	570	14.03.02-31.03.02	to Swiss International Air Lines
HB-JAV	574	19.03.02-31.03.02	to Swiss International Air Lines

* Embraer ERJ145LR with additional fuel capacity for longer range

Balair + CTA

The history of the new Balair began in June 1948, when the Basle-based section of the Swiss Aero-Club established a flight school at Sternenfeld-Birsfelden Aerodrome. When operations at Birsfelden ceased, the company moved to the new airport near Blotzheim, which had been opened in 1946. On 5 October 1952, the Basle electorate voted for the creation of a limited company and, on 6 January 1953, Balair was merged with Aviatik beider Basel to form Balair AG, with a capital of CHF 300,000, provided by the Kanton Basel-Stadt (Canton of Basle-City) (60 per cent) and Basel-Land (3 per cent). The remaining 37 per cent were held by private organisations and individuals. Professor Dr Hans Peter Tschudi was elected the first president. Activities were initially limited to flight training, aircraft maintenance, and handling of Swissair aircraft and those of other airlines at Basle-Mulhouse. Soon operations expanded to include sightseeing and air-taxi flights, whooping-cough flights, and aerial spraying in the cantons of Basle and Solothurn, and in Southern Germany. Among its motley fleet were the Cessna C.170, Piper L-4 Cub, Bücker Bü131 Jungmann, Piper Pa.12S Cruiser, and the DH.85 Leopard Moth.

The emerging inclusive-tour charter business offered new opportunities. The capital was increased to CHF 750,000 and, in May 1957, Balair acquired a Vickers 610 Viking 1B, HB-AAR, and added a second, HB-AAN, a year later, both from German carrier LTU, which were used to provide charter flights to the Mediterranean and destinations in Northern Europe. The Viking was a popular piston-engined airliner with British airlines, offering seating for 36 passengers and a range of 2,700 km at a speed of 340 km/h. Swissair too was keen to participate in the non-IATA charter business, which also offered an outlet for some of its surplus equipment. It bought into Balair on 28 January 1959, providing CHF 1.6 million of the new CHF 4 million capital for a 40 per cent holding. Also, as part of the framework agreement for the new collaboration, Swissair provided two four-engined Douglas DC-4 airliners, HB-ILA and HB-ILU, plus spares on generous terms. Balair thus became a de facto subsidiary of Swissair, which also became responsible for operational and technical matters and fleet procurement decisions. The advantage for Swissair was a relatively cheap entry into the charter business, while also satisfying the demands of the Basle region for a better participation in Swiss air transport.

The new DC-4 aircraft were delivered on 29 May and 10 April 1959 respectively and enabled Balair to expand into the long-haul market, with flights to the United States, South America, South Africa and India. Two more DC-4s, HB-ILB and ILC, followed in 1960, as did a popular eight-passenger de Havilland DH.104 Dove 6B, HB-LAQ named *Basler Dybli,* which was used for small passenger groups and for pilot training. However, 1960 had started badly. On 15 May, HB-ILA, having taken off from Khartoum on a ferry flight to Dakar, Senegal, crashed into the slope of Jebel Marr, near Tora-Tonga, still in Sudan, while cruising at an altitude of 2,450 m. All 12 crews perished in the accident, which has been blamed on a navigational error. The long-haul network was gradually expanded, made possible by the transfer of two larger Douglas DC-6B, HB-IBU and HB-IBZ, from Swissair, with another, HB-IBR, delivered in 1964.

CTA's sole MD-83 HB-IUI was operated briefly in 1992-1993 (Collection M Winter)

Balair sole de Havilland DH.104 Dove 6BA HB-LAQ (Barry Friend Collection)

Balair started operations with two Vickers VC.1 Viking 1B including HB-AAN

Douglas DC-4 photographed at Sion

Save the children

The new decade was also the start of many special humanitarian flights in support of the United Nations and the Geneva-based International Committee of the Red Cross (ICRC), starting with the Congo for the UN at the end of 1960. Over the next 20 years, Balair aircraft could be seen at various flashpoints across the world, including at Yemen in 1963 and during the Biafran War, one of the most vicious and bloodiest civil wars between Nigeria and the secessionist Biafra Republic between 1967 and 1970, during which more than one million people died in battle, with starvation, especially of children, claiming the vast majority of lives. Although the United Nations and most national governments were reluctant to become involved in what was seen as an internal conflict, various church groups and non-governmental organisations (NGOs) organised an airlift of food and medicine to overcome the naval, air and land blockade by the Nigerian Federal Military Government (FMG). Balair participated in the airlift in 1968/69 on behalf of the ICRC with a Transall C-160A, HB-ILN, leased from the German Government on 26 October 1968, which was delivered to its base at Santa Isabel (now Malabo) on the island of Fernando Pó (now Bioko, Equatorial Guinea) on 5 November, but was damaged at the Uli airstrip, Biafra, four days later, when taking 20 hits from Nigerian MiG-17 fighter jets. The Transall was returned to the German Government on 23 April 1970. Also used on the Biafran Airlift for ICRC were four USAF Boeing C-97G-25-BO Stratofreighters registered HB-ILW, HB-ILX, HB-ILY and HB-ILZ, from 8 April 1969 until the final surrender of Biafra on 12 January 1970. Other aircraft were the Douglas DC-6A/C, HB-IBU, Mitsubishi Mu-2B business jet, HB-LEB, and Beech 90 King Air, HB-GBK, all based at Santa Isabel, and three DC-6B, HB-IBR, HB-IBS and HB-IBT, operating out of Cotonou, Dahomey (now Benin). The flights were undertaken under cover of darkness and without lights to avoid Nigerian attack aircraft. Each aircraft made as many as four round-trips each night into Uli. DC-6B HB-IBT crashed on approach to the darkened Uli airstrip on 7 May 1969 and was completely destroyed, together with 10 tonnes of foodstuffs and medicine. Balair also assisted frequently in the Middle East (1967-1982), Central Africa (1970), East Pakistan (1971) and Vietnam and Angola in 1975.

Boeing Stratofreighter and Douglas DC-6 at Cotonou/ Cadjehoun (Marcel Tschudin/CRC)

Douglas DC-4 HB-ILB in Yemen (Hans Versell-Neuhaus)

Friendship operation

But all was not well. Top-heavy management, poor maintenance organisation, and inefficient performance per employee, plunged the airline into the red and led to a reduction in personnel. While its DC-4 and DC-6B aircraft were used to serve long-haul destinations and were uncompetitive on short-haul routes, this was partially improved with the acquisition of a Fokker F.27-200 Friendship twin-turboprop aircraft, HB-AAI, but this was damaged beyond repair on landing at Malaga on 13 September 1964. There were no casualties among the 45 occupants.

When Swissair decided in 1963 to stop its uneconomical services out of the capital Berne, it faced heavy criticism for neglecting its domestic network. Private company Globe Air petitioned the Federal authorities for a licence to re-instate this service, even without a subsidy, but Swissair insisted on its rights and tasked Balair to provide flights on its behalf. With the 365 m runway at Bern/Belpmoos inadequate for Swissair's smallest aircraft, it acquired two 44-seat Fokker F.27-400 Friendship twin-turboprop aircraft, HB-AAU and HB-AAV, to provide a connection between Bern and Zurich. After some improvements at the airport, the service

A small Fleet of Fokker F.27 Friendship twin turboprop aircraft were put on domestic services from Berne and Basle on behalf of Swissair, and below, the McDonnell Douglas DC-8-55F

to Zurich was resumed on 11 June 1965. Another service was opened between Basle and Geneva, although this proved less popular. Balair also added Berne-Paris and Basle-Frankfurt services. Two more Friendships were ordered by Swissair in March and December 1966, also for operation by Balair. The Friendship operation was given provisional approval until 31 October 1966, but this was later extended. The DC-4 was also used on European freight services for Swissair, which proved successful and persuaded Balair to acquire its own DC-4, registered HB-ILD.

To keep pace with its growing business, a capital increase became necessary, but, when in 1966 the Basle electorate declined to endorse additional funds, Balair had to go cap in hand to Swissair, which raised its stake to 48.9 per cent, but with 57 per cent voting rights. On 28 March 1968, Balair entered the jet age with a Convair 990A, HB-ICH,

leased from Swissair until 30 March 1971. It was operated mainly from Zurich, as it would have been weight-limited on take-off from Basle. Swissair continued to provide the maintenance of the aircraft during the lease period. Balair acquired its own Douglas DC-9-33F freighter, HB-IDN, from McDonnell Douglas on 17 April 1970, while a second aircraft, a DC-9-32 was transferred from Swissair on 18 September that same year. Swissair's decision to discontinue the scheduled Fokker services out of Basle and Berne in 1971 forced Balair into redundancies, especially of flight crew.

The fleet was further increased by a four-engined DC-8-55F jet, HB-IDU, bought from Flying Tigers and delivered on 2 April 1971, which replaced the Convair 990A, followed by a stretched 249-passenger DC-8-63PF, HB-IDZ, bought from Eastern Airlines on 1 May 1972.

Douglas DC-9-30

Convair 990A Coronado HB-ICH was leased from Swissair between 1968 and 1971

The necessary capital increase to CHF 32 million was entirely subscribed by Swissair, which secured it a majority holding of 56 per cent. In 1975, Balair inaugurated a cargo service with the DC-8-55 from Basle to Lagos, with an occasional stop at Palma di Mallorca. The next few years were determined by a massive rise in the price of oil, continuing currency problems and terrorist attacks on aircraft, which depressed traffic and forced Balair into a retrenchment. The charter tariffs on the North Atlantic came under particular pressure. However, Balair was able to keep its head above water and, in 1976, revenues exceeded CHJF 100 million for the first time. Good income was generated by flights to the Far East, especially to Bangkok and Colombo, to Nairobi in East Africa, and to Rio de Janeiro in Brazil. North America also witnessed an improvement, with New York and Los Angeles added in 1974. A DC-8-62CF, HB-IDH, which was a long-range convertible passenger/freight version, was

leased from Swissair on 1 April 1976. In passenger service, it was configured for 152 passengers.

As charter traffic continued its upward trend, Basle started to lose out, as flights were gradually transferred to Zurich, partially because travel agents preferred to offer flights from Zurich/Kloten, but also because it made economic sense for Balair and Swissair to operate from the same location. Basle was largely reduced to handling activities, with only the last DC-6B operating and being maintained at the city. A loan of CHF 20 million enabled Balair to acquire a brand-new McDonnell Douglas DC-10-30, HB-IHK, on 31 January 1979, which remained in service until 15 January 1993.

The year 1979 was a high point in Balair's history, with record revenues of CHF 183 million and 737,000 passengers. It was not to last. The oil price soared once again, long-haul routes were no longer profitable, and on intra-European flights, charter airlines were being pushed out by

McDonnell Douglas DC-8-63PF HB-IDZ at Malta (John Visanich)

The McDonnell Douglas MD-80 was operated between 1982 and 1995

A sole three-engined McDonnell Douglas DC-10-30 HB-IHK entered service in early 1979

McDonnell Douglas DC-8 and DC-9 aircraft at Zurich/Kloten

scheduled airlines. Balair sold two aircraft, ceased flights to San Francisco, Miami, Lima and seven destinations in the Caribbean, made 16 per cent of staff redundant, and tried to hedge its fuel costs, which all contributed to small profits.

These were further improved between 1986 and 1989, as oil prices fell back again and the US dollar weakened. Flights were once again increased to North America, partly under contract to Swissair, and other growing destinations were

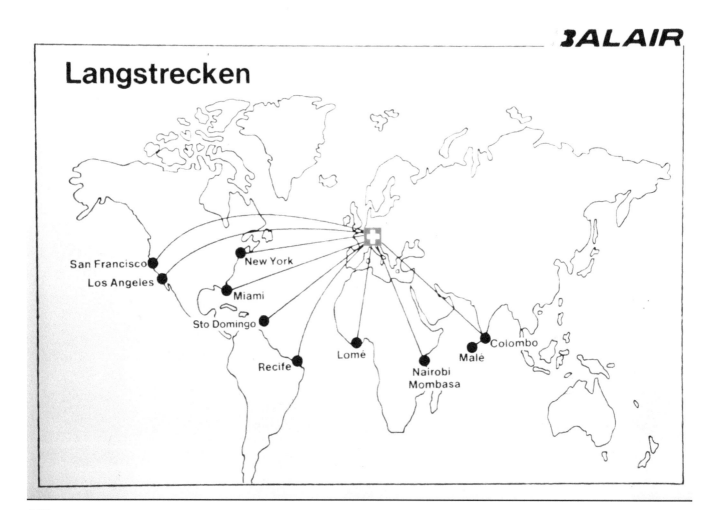

The A310-300 twinjet was fitted out for 220 passengers

A310-300 HB-IPL in attractive new colours

Sud-Aviation Caravelle 10R HB-ICQ was previously operated by SATA

Thailand, the Maldives, Sri Lanka and Kenya, as well as shorter flights to Spain, Greece and Turkey. The fleet was boosted by small numbers of Douglas DC-9-30, MD-80 and Airbus A310-200 aircraft. For a time, Balair gained authorisation from the Italian authorities to provide flights out of Milan to the Maldives, Kenya and the Caribbean. The Gulf War and its aftermath again resulted in losses. With the delivery of two new A310-300s, HB-IPL and HB-IPM, Balair introduced a new paintscheme highlighting the wings in yellow overall.

Charter anomaly

The anomaly of having a financial interest in two charter airlines was removed on 1 January 1993, when Swissair amalgamated Balair and CTA under the new name, BalairCTA AG, with Swissair's shareholding now 99.6 per cent. For political reasons, the registered office of the new company was in Geneva and the accounting department

in Basle, but the operational base was moved to Zurich. Despite restructuring and mass redundancies, and good business on flights to North America, the Dominican Republic, Maldives and Thailand, and within Europe to Spain, the Canary Islands and Cyprus, the charter business was unprofitable. The unfavourable cost structure and the increasing overlap of charter and scheduled flights, made the operation of a pure charter company no longer rational. Operations were discontinued on 31 October 1995, and short-haul operations were transferred to Crossair, together with four MD-81/83 aircraft, with long-haul operations taken over by Swissair, together with three A310-300. The name BalairCTA continued to be used on long-haul flights, which provided regular services from Zurich to Anchorage, Miami, Orlando, Puerto Plata, Punta Cana, San Francisco and Varadero in the Americas, south to Mombasa, and eastwards to Colombo, Phuket and the Maldives.

Geneva/Cointrin-based CTA-Compagnie de Transport

McDonnell Douglas MD-87 HB-IUD

McDonnell Douglas MD-87 HB-IUB taking off from Zurich

Aérien had been founded by Swissair on 28 October 1978 from the assets of another charter airline at Geneva, Société Anonyme de Transport Aérien (SATA), which had been established on 29 June 1966 by Raymond Lambert, Charles Jacquat and the Geneva Aero Club with a starting capital of CHF 60,000, but ceased operations on 23 August 1978. In the intervening years, SATA had become the largest independent carrier in Switzerland, using Douglas DC-8, McDonnell Douglas MD-80 and Sud-Aviation Caravelle 10R jets on charter and inclusive-tour flights within Europe

Boeing 757-200 narrow-body twinjet with green Balair titles

and to the Americas and the Caribbean. It also used light aircraft on air-taxi and alpine experience flights including glacier landings. CTA took over some of the personnel and the three Sud-Aviation SE-210 Caravelle 10R twinjets, HB-ICN, HB-ICO and HB-ICQ, and started flying on 2 November 1978. These were used largely on charter flights to the Mediterranean, North Africa, Greece, Turkey and the Canary Islands. Several cantons in the west of Switzerland bought into the airline in 1979. Some 10 per cent of its activities came from ad-hoc flights, for which one Caravelle was fitted out luxuriously for executive transport.

Plans were made to acquire the Fokker 100 to replace the Caravelles, but the airline opted instead for the McDonnell Douglas MD-87, placing an order for four aircraft on 19 December 1986. Its decision was most likely in recognition that both Swissair, which held a 38.3 per cent stake but 52 per cent voting rights, and Balair already operated the MD-80. The first MD-87, HB-IUA, configured with 125 seats, a notable increase in capacity, operated its first CTA service on 30 April 1988 with a flight from Zurich to Antalya in Turkey. The airline expanded its premium offer by dividing the cabin and fitting out the front with its own luxury environment. Charter flights were undertaken principally to the Balearic and Canary Islands, and Greece, as well as flights to Naples and Palermo. Sub-charters and scheduled services were also flown for Swissair, which at times generated some 40 per cent of its income. Two MD-87 were leased to Swissair in March 1992 for scheduled services during weekdays, among them to Amsterdam and Birmingham. CTA found a niche and was profitable throughout, except in 1979. It did not pursue a growth strategy and was easily assimilated into Balair.

Surprisingly, Swissair once again entered the long-haul charter business with the establishment of a new company, Balair/CTA Leisure AG, which started flying on 1 November 1997 with two A310-300. Important to the re-establishment and development of the charter arm was the use of its own pilots and cabin crew with lower salary. The main focus was on destinations in North America, the Caribbean, the Indian Ocean and East Africa, but Balair/CTA was also tasked with offering tailor-made flights for companies, organisations and private individuals. Aircraft carried only Balair titles. On short and medium-haul routes, two Boeing 757-200, HB-IHR and HB-IHS, were operated exclusively for tour operator Hotelplan and its subsidiaries. Balair also had two new Boeing 767-300ER, HB-IHV and HB-IHW, as well as two leased from Air Europe, for long-haul operations. However, the failure of Swissair also signalled the end of Balair/CTA, which made its last flight on 5 October 2001. Hotelplan took over the two Boeing 757-200s and formed a new company, Belair Airlines AG, on 16 October. Belair started operations from Zurich to Mediterranean resort areas on 3 November 2001.

Four Balair 767-300ER were used on long-haul services from 1999 but all operations ceased on 5 October 2001

Balair/BalairCTA Fleet 1957-2001

All dates from 1 January 1993 are for BalairCTA

Vickers VC.1 Viking 1B 1957-1963 (2)

24-passenger short-range aircraft, powered by two 1,260 kW (1,690 hp) Bristol Hercules 634 radial engines, generating a cruising speed of 340 km/h

HB-AAN		219	01.05.58-07.02.63	ex D-BARI; to Air Ferry as G-AIVF
HB-AAR		217	29.06.57-04.02.63	ex D-ADAM; to Air Ferry as G-AIVD

Douglas DC-4/C-54 1959-1970 (5)

40-passenger low-wing, all-metal monoplane powered by four 1,082 kW (1,450 hp) Pratt & Whitney R-2000-2SD13-G Twin Wasp engines, generating a maximum speed of 450 km/h

HB-ILA	DC-4-1009	43072	29.05.59-15.05.60	ex Swissair; crashed into Jebel Massa, Sudan
HB-ILB	C-54A-15-DC	10359	20.12.60-02.01.64	ex N75415; to Air Ferry as G-ASOG
HB-ILC	C-54A-10-DC	10335	17.06.60-31.01.63	ex N88922; to Air Ferry as G-ASFY
HB-ILD	DC-4-1009	42995	30.01.67-08.09.70	ex SX-DAG; to Congofrigo as 9Q-CWJ
HB-ILU	C-54E-5-DO	27289	10.04.59-09.12.69	ex Swissair; to Aer Turas Teoranto as EI-ARS

de Havilland DH.104 Dove 6B 1960-1968 (1)

Eight-passenger short-haul monoplane, powered by two 250 kW (330 hp) de Havilland Gipsy Queen 70 engines, generating a cruising speed of 300 km/h

HB-LAQ	*Basler Dybli*	4338	04.02.60-09.07.68	ex G-AODN; to ..as CF-GAA

Fokker F.27 Friendship 1964-1995 (6)

56-seat short/medium-range high-wing aircraft, powered by two 1,678 kW (2,250 hp) Rolls-Royce Dart Mk.532-7 turboprop engines, generating a speed of 460km/h

HB-AAI	F.27-200	10141	02.04.64-12.09.64	ex PH-IOP; damaged beyond repair on landing at Malaga
HB-AAU	F.27-200	10200	10.11.64-31.10.71	ex D-BAKE; to NLM as PH-KFC
HB-AAV	F.27-200	10276	04.12.64-31.10.71	to NLM as PH-KFD
HB-AAW	F.27-400	10323	30.03.66-31.10.71	to Gulf Aviation as A40-FD
HB-AAX	F.27-400	10351	10.02.67-31.10.71	to NLM as PH-KFE
HB-AAZ	F.27-400	10268	17.09.73-22.12.95	ex F-BRQL; stored at Woensdrecht, Netherlands

Douglas DC-6 1964-1972 (4)

68-passenger, low-wing monoplane, powered by four 1,865 kW (2,500 hp) Pratt & Whitney R-2800-CB17 Double Wasp engines, generating a speed of 510 km/h

HB-IBR	DC-6B	44165/400	19.06.64-00.03.69	ex SE-BDT; witdrawn from us and broken up 04.03.70
HB-IBS	DC-6A	45531/1015	14.01.69-08.07.82	ex G-APNO; to Conair as C-GIBS

| HB-IBT | DC-6A/C | 45532/1025 | 12.01.69-06.05.69 | ex G-APNP; crashed on approach to Uli airstrip, Biafra |
| HB-IBW | DC-6A | 43296/200 | 19.01.72-04.09.72 | ex D-ABAZ; leased from Jet Aviation |

Douglas C-47B 1967-1974 (1)

21-passengers low-wing, all-metal monoplane, powered by two 895 kW (1,200 hp) Pratt & Whitney R-1830-S1C3G Twin Wasp engines, generating a speed of 370 km/h

| HB-ITD | | 16465/33213 | 26.10.67-29.03.74 | ex PH-MAA; to Air Transport Inc as N37737 |

Convair 990A Coronado 1968-1971 (1)

130-passenger narrowbody aircraft, powered by four 71.4 kN (16,050 lb) General Electric CJ805-23B turbofan engines, generating a speed of 1,000 km/h

| HB-ICH | | 30-10-17 | 28.03.68-30.03.71 | leased from Swissair |

Douglas DC-9-30 1970-1988 (3)

115-passenger short/medium-range aircraft, powered by two rear-mounted 64.5 kN (14,500 lb) Pratt & Whitney JT9D-9 turbofan engines, generating a speed of 895 km/h

HB-IDN	DC-9-33CF	47465/584	19.04.70-31.10.76	to McDonnell Douglas as N7465B 07.11.76
HB-IDT	DC-9-34LR	47711/844	06.11.76-18.01.85	to Ozark Airlines as N936L
HB-IFZ	DC-9-32	47479/605	18.05.79-02.06.88	ex Swissair; to Northwest Airlines as N985US

Douglas DC-8-55CF 1971-1979 (1)

189-passenger long-range aircraft, powered by four 80.6 kN (18,200 lb) Pratt & Whitney JT3D-3B turbofan engines, generating a speed of 865 km/h

| HB-IDU | | 45817/248 | 08.01.71-01.10.79 | ex N805U; to Overseas National Airways (ONA) as N9110V |

McDonnell Douglas DC-8-60 1972-1985 (2)

189-passenger long-range aircraft, powered by four 80.6 kN (18,200 lb) Pratt & Whitney JT3D-3B turbofan engines, generating a speed of 865 km/h

| HB-IDH | DC-8-62CF | 45984/370 | 02.03.76-00.12.81 | ex Swissair; to Fuerza Aérea del Peru as FAP371 |
| HB-IDZ | DC-8-63PF | 46074/498 | 02.05.72-29.10.85 | ex N8760; to United Parcel Service (UPS) as N874UP 02.12.85 |

McDonnell Douglas DC-10-30 1979-1993 (1)

270-passenger long-range wide-body aircraft, powered by three 227 kN (51,000 lb) General Electric CF6-50C turbofan engines, generating a speed of 895 km/h

| HB-IHK | | 46998/267 | 31.01.79-15.01.93 | to Martinair Holland as PH-MCO |

McDonnell Douglas MD-80 1982-1995 (7)

172-seat short/medium-range aircraft, powered by two rear-mounted 89 kN (20,000 lb) Pratt & Whitney JT8D-217A turbofan engines, generating a speed of 875 km/h

HB-INB	49101/1051	01.04.82-01.03.95	leased from Swissair
HB-INR	49277/1181	01.02.85-19.12.95	to Crossair
HB-INW	49569/1405	18.09.87-05.11.95	to Crossair
HB-ISZ	49930/1720	20.06.90-02.11.95	to Crossair
HB-IUI	49710/1547	01.01.93-17.11.93	ex CTA; to Venus Airlines as SX-BAQ
HB-IUK	49398/1332	12.03.95-01.10.95	ex SE-DPS; to Swissair
HB-IUL	49442/1358	21.03.95-01.10.95	ex SE-DRU; to Swissair

Airbus A310-300 1986-1999 (4)

220-passenger medium/long-range wide-body aircraft, powered by two 222 kN (50,000 lb) Pratt & Whitney JT9D-7R4E1 turbofan engines, generating a cruising speed of 850 km/h

HB-IPK	*Liestal*	412	21.03.86-01.02.93	to Swissair
HB-IPL		640	27.04.92-16.12.99	to Oman Air as A40-OC
HB-IPM		642	30.04.92-25.11.99	to Oman Air asA40-OD
HB-IPN		672	19.05.93-25.01.96	to Swissair

McDonnell Douglas MD-87 1993-1995 (4)

130-passenger medium-range narrow-body aircraft, powered by two 89 kN (20,000 lb) rear-mounted Pratt & Whitney JT*D-217C trubofan engines, generating a maximum cruising speed of 870 km/h

HB-IUA	49585/1457	01.01.93-15.11.95	ex CTA; to SAS as LN-RMX
HB-IUB	49586/1472	01.01.93-15.11.95	ex CTA; to SAS as LN-RMY
HB-IUC	49587/1541	01.01.93-01.11.95	ex CTA; to Reno Air as N753RA
HB-IUD	49641/1617	01.01.93-28.11.95	ex CTA; to Reno Air as N754RA

Boeing 767-300ER 1999-2001 (4)

290-passenger medium/long-range wide-body aircraft, powered by two 252 kN (56,650 lb) Pratt & Whitney PW 4000 turbofan engines, generating a speed of 900 km/h

HB-IHT	26387/445	02.10.99-01.10.00	ex EI-CJA; to Canadian Airlines as C-GHLA
HB-IHU	26388/456	28.10.99-29.11.00	ex EI-CJB; to Canadian Airlines as C-GHLK
HB-IHV	30564/798	11.08.00-05.10.01	stored; to Sobelair as OO-IHV 28.06.02
HB-IHW	30565/802	26.09.00-05.10.01	stored; to Ethiopian Airlines as ET-ALH 16.01.02

Boeing 757-200 2000-2001 (2)

220-passenger medium-range narrow-body aircraft, powered by two 193 kN (43,500 lb) Rolls-Royce RB211-535E4 eturbofan engines, generating a cruising speed of 855 km/h

HB-IHR	29379/919	19.04.00-05.10.01	stored
HB-IHS	30394/922	28.04.00-05.10.01	to Belair as HB-HIS 31.10.01

CTA Fleet 1978-1993

Sud-Aviation SE-210 Caravelle 10R 1978-1989 (4)

118-passenger short/medium-range narrow-body aircraft, powered by two 62.3 kN (14,000 lb) rear-mounted Pratt & Whitney JT8D turbofan engines, generating a cruising speed of 825 km/h

HB-ICI		250	12.12.80-26.06.89	ex EC-BRJ; to Istanbul Airlines as TC-ALA
HB-ICN	*Ville de Genève*	253	28.10.78-31.05.88	ex SATA; to Istanbul Airlines as TC-ABA
HB-ICO	*Romandie*	255	01.11.78-20.12.88	ex SATA; to Air Service Nantes as F-GGKD
HB-ICQ		222	28.10.78-01.12.87	ex SATA; to Istanbul Airlines as TC-ASA

McDonnell Douglas MD-83 1992-1993 (1)

172-seat short/medium-range aircraft, powered by two rear-mounted 89 kN (20,000 lb) Pratt & Whitney JT8D-217A turbofan engines, generating a speed of 875 km/h

HB-IUI	49710/1547	24.03.92-01.01.93	ex XA-TOR; to BalairCTA

McDonnell Douglas MD-87 1988-1993 (4)

130-passenger medium-range narrow-body aircraft, powered by two 89 kN (20,000 lb) rear-mounted Pratt & Whitney JT8D-217C trubofan engines, generating a maximum cruising speed of 870 km/h

HB-IUA	49585/1457	01.04.88-01.01.93	to BalairCTA
HB-IUB	49586/1472	13.05.88-01.01.93	to BalairCTA
HB-IUC	49587/1541	16.12.88-01.01.93	to BalairCTA
HB-IUD	49641/1617	18.08.89-01.01.93	to BalairCTA

Milton Keynes UK
Ingram Content Group UK Ltd.
UKHW051626280224
438371UK00013B/87